Her Silver-Tongued Companion

To my family and friends, with gratitude for their support and encouragement all these years

Harryette Mullen

Her Silver-Tongued Companion

Reading Poems by Harryette Mullen

Harryette Mullen

Edited by Georgina Colby

EDINBURGH
University Press

Edinburgh University Press is one of the leading university presses in the UK. We publish academic books and journals in our selected subject areas across the humanities and social sciences, combining cutting-edge scholarship with high editorial and production values to produce academic works of lasting importance. For more information visit our website: edinburghuniversitypress.com

Published with the support of the University of Edinburgh Scholarly Publishing Initiatives Fund.

Edinburgh University Press Ltd
13 Infirmary Street
Edinburgh, EH1 1LT

First published in hardback by Edinburgh University Press 2024

Typeset in 11/13pt Adobe Sabon by
Cheshire Typesetting Ltd, Cuddington, Cheshire

A CIP record for this book is available from the British Library

ISBN 978 1 3995 2360 8 (hardback)
ISBN 978 1 3995 3335 5 (paperback)
ISBN 978 1 3995 2361 5 (webready PDF)
ISBN 978 1 3995 2362 2 (epub)

Contents

Figures

Acknowledgements

Editing this Critical Edition of Harryette Mullen's work has been an honour, and a truly wonderful experience. It has been a close collaboration between Harryette and me from start to finish. I cannot thank Harryette enough for contributing her work to the series and collaborating on the volume with such care and generosity.

We would like to thank the artist Lorna Simpson for granting permission to exhibit *Jet Mississippi* (2012) on the front cover of this book. Simpson's collages of vintage photographs from *Ebony* and *Jet* recall a hopeful era when African Americans' social, political, and economic aspirations were reflected in magazines published by John H. Johnson. His decision to publish a photograph of the murdered Emmett Till amplified the voice of Emmett's mother, Mamie Till-Mobley, adding momentum to the civil rights movement.

This Critical Edition would not have been possible without the kindness of the presses who have published Harryette's works. We would like to thank Graywolf Press for their exceptional generosity in granting permissions to reproduce poems from the collections *Urban Tumbleweed: Notes from a Tanka Diary* (2013) and *Recyclopedia* (2006). Our deepest thanks also go to University of California Press for granting permissions to reproduce selections from *Sleeping with the Dictionary* (2002).

This collection of Harryette's poems is complemented by the rich scholarship in the Critical Essays section. Our heartfelt thanks go to Lee Ann Brown, Solveig Daugaard, Alan Gilbert, Emily Greenwood, Daniel Kane, and Ayesha

Ramachandran for their time and thoughtfulness in contributing their insightful readings and remarkable knowledge of Harryette's work to the volume.

Our thanks go to the brilliant team at Edinburgh University Press who supported this volume from proposal to book production: Emily Sharp, Elizabeth Fraser, and Bekah Dey.

Preface: Harryette Mullen's Deep Play: Oulipo for Everybody and Then Some

Lee Ann Brown

How can we survive if we cannot play together?

When asked to write this preface, my mind immediately went to the personal and anecdotal in my interactions with Harryette Mullen's work and her delightful self. And that is no accident. Harryette Mullen's deeply unique work weaves poetry from language both high and low, to all in between, code switching to make dwellings for new ways of thinking, speaking, playing, working, of being together, and is a vital curative for what ails this world.

Mullen's wildly innovative practices have a down-to-earth element. She has often generously parsed out how she wrote many of her works, in comments that feel like an instruction manual or experiment list for other people to become poets, with encouraging "you can do this too" generosity. In addition to this ground-breaking new gathering of her work, I want to give a shout-out to Mullen and Henning's sourcebook *Looking Up Harryette Mullen*, an epistolary dialogic work proposed by Barbara Henning which lends itself to the back-and-forth mouth and mind music of Harryette Mullen's vastly inventive practice, and Mullen's own book of essays and interviews, *The Cracks Between What We Are and What We Are Supposed to Be* for further elucidation as to her sources and methods.

Mullen's highly inventive and intertextual work is in dialogue with everyone from Basho, who inspired her reinvention of the tanka into a thirty-one syllable form with variable line lengths, in which she reinvents a way for poetry to help her learn a new landscape by walking in Los Angeles, to Sapphire, and Sappho, to new practices of visual collage, even sometimes using genealogical material.

Mullen's wordplay invites the reader into a reciprocal game of cat's cradle – being passed between two hands, the strings are made of words, and function at a high level of call and response with intimate and vast overlapping cultural and vernacular reference. I think of the associative wordplay that dwells in formative children's rhymes, songs, and games. The song "Say say, oh playmate, come out and play with me" (and all its permutational variations such as "Say say, Oh Hippie," or "Say Say, Oh Monster") is one Mullen surely came across either in her Texas childhood, or in her extensive folkloric and literary research on the complex musicality and referential power of nursery rhymes and their relationship to poetry. The way these parodic play party rhymes morph into the situation or community at hand were sung together at the summer camps I attended growing up in the South.

Her practice connects nascent human creativity with sophisticated poetic processes like the experimental tendencies of the "Language Poets" in the Bay Area, and movements and societies such as the Oulipians (more in league with the rebellious Noulipians), undercutting doctrinaire exclusivity that often is associated with pressure cooker coteries. Mullen's work stands for wonder, pleasure, and the way these language games generate poems fully open to possibility of serious play with the reader/playmate. Many so-called Language Poets in her spheres studied with or attended lectures by the linguistic theorist George Lakoff and applied his proposition that a language can be defined as a vocabulary plus a set of rules. What does that mean for poetry? Every poem could be seen as a new and different language with its own vocabulary and set of rules. These views and practices liberate the poem – which is art made out of words – from the mire of simple "aboutness" and launch it into a space of seeing what the poem can DO.

The thing I love about Harryette's work is her singular, rebellious spirit of making up and breaking the rules as she composes her word collages and dictionary games. In the line, "A postcard of fidelity shaking hands with earnest money" ("Drinking Mojitos in Cuba Libre") is her own kind of free form (n)oulipian Noun + 7. I picture the famous photo of Fidel Castro and Ernest Hemingway shaking hands.

My encounter with onion skin pages hooked me on playing in the big dictionary and the bibiliomantic practice of associative concepts and the interlinked "wreading" and "riting" practices, allowing the web of systematic and associational source material to come into my work, playing on the vibrational spider web of language.

This delight, this wild, free-form play with language at hand is the generous and generative heart of what Harryette Mullen's poetry gives best. I puzzle over the relationship of these foundational singings learned in community, and their primarily oral literacies that reread and rewrite received language material in relation to contemporary, avant-garde, and experimental poetry.

When I encountered Harryette Mullen's work through her manuscript, *Trimmings*, I felt welcomed into her field of play. In the spring of 1986, Roberto Bedoya, then the Artistic Director of Intersection for the Arts in San Francisco, heard I had started a press with the name Tender Buttons, dedicated to publishing experimental poetry by women "under the sign of Stein." He recommended I look at Harryette's manuscript which refigured and undercut Stein's methods in her long poetic sequence *Tender Buttons*. Harryette focused on the language of women's clothing, and the often-sexualized language to describe it, such as "fur-below." She forged a new syntax in relation to Stein's text that goes far beyond simple imitation. In the notes included with the original publication of *Trimmings*, she describes her project as "A way to think about women and language." This intersectional description is at the heart of why I love her work: there is a thinking that is subversive and joyful in its investigative play, replete with both pleasure and critique. It's inherent in her diction, her "diction-aerie" is a nested bed, each book an extended garden.

The poems in this volume make clear the roots of her accomplishment – the exposure of quadruple exclusions while bridging the gaps and writing across the aisle of experimentation and identity politics. I am in awe of the nerve and smarts Harryette possesses to have created work that crosses so many intersections of contemporary poetic practice and complicates (in a good way) the sometimes reductive stance of poetry that is solely identity-based.

Everybody's always got their own relationship to the text, especially with one as open and inviting to interpretation as these, and I am so glad to have these new and astute critical articles to add to the growing body of Mullen Studies! Long may she write and sing and be read and may we her expanded readership be her "Silver-tongued Companions," singing alongside her practice.

* * *

This morning I woke from a dream of how making a poem is like a Katamari video game in which your avatar is this little ball that rolls around the room of your mind and picks up more and more attractive objects, as it rolls, turning into a larger and larger sticky ball of colorful stuff or words in this case. A kind of "magpie poetics" mapping itself around the room of the poem. This reminds me of Harryette Mullen's inventive poetics of radical play which renews and strengthens the essential human capacity to play and create which is everyone's birthright.

* * *

I am so excited to see this and look forward to the even wider reception and "stirrings up" her playful and subversive work will create as it reaches a wider, international audience. Thank you to everyone who made this collection happen, especially, of course, Harryette Mullen.

Introduction: Imagined Readers

Georgina Colby

I beg to dicker with my silver-tongued companion, whose
lips are ready to read my shining gloss.

Harryette Mullen, 'Sleeping with the Dictionary'

When Harryette Mullen titled this Critical Edition *Her Silver-Tongued Companion*, she extended an invitation to the reader
to join the intimate friendship between poet and language. It
is no coincidence that the phrase is lifted from the poem that
is widely considered to be Mullen's *ars poetica*, as Al Filreis
has observed, and the eponymous poem of one of her most
renowned collections, *Sleeping with the Dictionary* (2002).[1]
In this poem the poet lies with the dictionary as a lover,
her wordplay substituting the provocative 'dicker' for the
expected 'differ', evoking the persuasive tongue of her literary
companion, creating a symbiotic relation between the lips of
the poet and the 'gloss' of the dictionary. The cerebral pleasure
of the couple, both 'aroused by myriad possibilities' in lan-
guage, trying out 'the most perverse positions in the practice
of our nightly act, the penetration of the denotative body of
the work' brings the reader to the core of Mullen's poetry. It
is pleasure yielded by experiment, and serious rumination on
the art of poetry. In an interview for *The New York Times*,
Claudia Rankine listed Mullen's *Sleeping with the Dictionary*
as her favourite book to assign with her students. Drawing

1

on Mullen's own comments on her practice of working with 'ready-mades from the mass-culture dumpster' Rankine observes that the reader of Mullen's work 'encounters, in an improvisatory manner, folk sermons, raps, puns, riddles, political slogans, advertisements, headlines, etc.' The work, Rankine comments, 'refuses to identify with a single person, place, or thing as it engages race in America'. For Rankine, Mullen's *Sleeping with the Dictionary* 'performs how a formally innovative text stays current with the culture, despite its publication date'.[2] This Critical Edition brings to light the ways in which Harryette Mullen's genre-defying work is central to our reflections on our present moment.

Who is the reader invited by Mullen into the relationship between book and poet? 'I write, optimistically, for an imagined audience of known and unknown readers', Mullen states in her essay 'Imagining the Unimagined Reader: Writing to the Unborn and Including the Excluded'.[3] One pathway into the pluralism of Mullen's writing is via the poet's comments on the diversity and inclusiveness of writing: 'I desire that my work appeals to an audience that is diverse and inclusive while at the same time wondering if human beings will ever learn how to be inclusive without repressing human diversity through cultural and linguistic imperialism.' The repression of human diversity through cultural and linguistic imperialism, attention to this, and the overcoming of this through literary experiment, is an element of Mullen's work and criticism that has been highly influential, informing the practices of many of her peers and contemporaries such as Claudia Rankine and Caroline Bergvall, among many others. Mullen explains: 'Not when I am writing, but after I have written, I consider who would be left out and excluded from the poem. Although it is not necessary or possible to include everyone, I find that it is useful to me as a writer to think about the fact that language, culture, and poetry always exclude as they include potential audiences.' This concern underpins the resistance to singularity in Mullen's poetry. 'One reason I have avoided a singular style or voice for my poetry is the possibility of including a diverse audience of readers attracted to different poems and different aspects of the work', Mullen remarks. 'I try' she states, 'to leave room for the unknown readers I can only imagine.'[4]

In the same essay, Mullen discusses the barriers to her work. Illiteracy and poverty are foremost, and the most pressing barriers, socially and politically, to overcome. Mullen's feminist vision of her future reader is imbricated with the surmounting of such inequalities: 'A future reader of my work is the offspring of an illiterate woman', Mullen states, remarking that 'A significant percentage of the world's population remains illiterate, the majority of them girls and women. An even greater number have minimal access to books or the leisure to read them.'[5] Mullen is not immune to or naively unaware of the paradox that haunts her work. On the contrary, Mullen is very explicit about the contradictory nature of her desires as a poet:

> I aspire to write poetry that would leave no insurmountable obstacle to comprehension and pleasure other than the ultimate limits of the reader's interest and linguistic competence. However, I do not necessarily approach this goal by applying a beautiful, pure, simple, or accessible literary language or by maintaining a clear, consistent, recognizable, or authentic voice in my work.

These discrepant desires operate as pluralising tensions in Mullen's work. For Mullen, writing is 'a process that is synthetic rather than organic, artificial rather than natural, human rather than divine'. Mullen states her inclination 'is to pursue what is minor, what is marginal, idiosyncratic, trivial, debased, or aberrant' in the language she speaks and writes.[6]

Mullen's essays offer crucial reflections on the political and literary contexts of her works, as well as her own philosophies and practices as an avant-garde writer. Mullen's body of critical work offers both a new theorisation of African American avant-garde writing and significant interventions into existing critical narratives in the field of avant-garde writing. As Hank Lazer comments in the Introduction to Mullen's essay collection, *The Cracks Between What We Are and What We Are Supposed To Be*, Mullen, writing in the era of identity politics, 'is determined to challenge over simplified versions of identity'.[7] Through creating an inclusive and open linguistic environment, Lazer observes: 'Mullen is helping us all to imagine and inhabit a multiethnic culture that has rid itself of xenophobia.'[8] Lazer remarks on the publication of Mullen's essays as a significant literary event, noting that Mullen's essays and interviews, like her poetry, 'are written at several key intersections: speech and writing, innovation and race'. *Her Silver-Tongued Companion* is designed to complement that collection of essays as the first full collected works of Mullen's poetry to date.

Mullen's work is foundational to an understanding of contemporary avant-garde writing for the intervention it makes in renegotiating the positioning of avant-garde poets whose works have been underrepresented. In her essay, 'Poetry and Identity', Mullen discusses the particular challenges that formally innovative minority poets experience in terms of publication and inclusion in literary groupings. For Mullen, writing in 2012, 'it would seem that representative "black" poets are currently more assimilable into the "mainstream" than "formally innovative" poets of any hue'.[9] Mullen notes: 'In the anthology and textbook markets poets "of color", given their automatic representational status, have a distinct advantage over "formally innovative" poets, who appeal to no large or easily identifiable demographic segment of the literary market.'[10] Mullen remarks that 'avant-garde' poets tend to be packaged for largely academic consumption in the same manner that 'poets of color' or 'spoken word' practitioners have been labelled and gathered into anthologies aimed at both mainstream and academic audiences. However, Mullen understands the avant-garde poet of color to threaten 'the cohesiveness of narratives that allow the mainstream audience to recognize, comprehend, or imagine a collective identity, purpose, and aesthetics for a literary group or movement.' Mullen observes:

> formally innovative minority poets, when visible at all, are
> not likely to be perceived either as typical of a racial/ethnic

group or as representative of an aesthetic movement. Their unaccountable existence therefore strains the seams of the critical narratives necessary to make them (individually and collectively) comprehensible and thus teachable and marketable. In each generation the erasure of the anomalous black writer abets the construction of a continuous, internally consistent tradition, and it deprives the idiosyncratic minority artist of a history, compelling her to struggle even harder to construct a cultural context out of her own radical individuality. She is unanticipated and often unacknowledged because of the imposed obscurity of her aesthetic antecedents.[11]

I have cited Mullen at length here because these comments not only provide insights into the poet's own journey to recognition but also offer a critical understanding of the publishing landscape for underrepresented poets in the twenty-first century. Of her own work, Mullen states that her first work, *Tree Tall Woman* (Energy Earth, 1981), enabled her to be positioned in the category of 'representational blackness' alongside the categories of 'feminist' and 'regional' poet. Her second and third published books, *Trimmings* (Tender Buttons, 1991) and *S*PeRM**K*T* (Singing Horse, 1992), were received as 'formally innovative'. For this reason, Mullen explains, these works of prose poetry were overlooked by those literary critics and publishers looking to place Mullen in an African American poetic tradition. Evie Shockley's landmark work *Renegade Poetics* is designed to tackle concerns by poets such as Mullen 'about ways that African American critical traditions have excluded exciting, significant, and innovative writing, specifically with regard to African American poetry'.[12] Shockley focuses on Mullen's polyvocality. Alongside Gwendolyn Brooks and Sonia Sanchez, Shockley positions Mullen as a black woman who has had to 'speak dialogically'. As writers, Shockley argues, Brooks, Sanchez, and Mullen 'exercise this skill by innovatively manipulating the formal elements of their poetry, so that works might be heard differently by different listeners'.[13] Shockley provides an in-depth analysis of

Mullen's experience and poetic responses to traversing the grounds of the varying readerships her works attract and the problems of literary categorising in the landscape of contemporary literature.

Mullen's poetry reveals the inseparability of blackness and formal innovation. Anthony Reed has determined the significance of this intricacy in Mullen's work for its philosophical questioning of meaning and form. For Reed, Mullen creates 'an abstracted blues poetics rooted in a form of irony as a nondialectical conception of difference, affirming the groundlessness of meaning and form'.[14] Reed's understanding offers insight into the reforming nature of Mullen's avant-garde practice. 'Blues irony', Reed observes, 'wears its mask *as* a mask of living language', allowing Mullen as poet 'to vacillate between recognizable critique and affirmation'.[15] Reed's close attention to Mullen's techniques grasps the political importance of Mullen's experiments, which for Reed: 'mark something other than a straightforward political project of mastering the other's language or giving voice to others'. Significantly, Reed states: 'Her work undoes hierarchies between the paradigmatic and the syntagmatic (and between black and experimental) and thereby challenges the limitations of allowable thought.'[16] The poems gathered in this volume have been carefully curated to amplify Mullen's poetic experiments and techniques.

Publishing Contexts: From *Tree Tall Woman* to *Open Leaves*

For Mullen, the other primary barriers to readers of her poetry other than illiteracy and poverty are 'availability and language'.[17] Mullen's works have largely been published in small editions by small presses and distributed via mail order and the Small Press Distribution in Berkeley. This Critical Edition makes a comprehensive collection of Mullen's works available widely for the first time. The tripartite curation of poems in this Critical Edition is designed to offer the most comprehensive collection of Mullen's work to date. The first part of the volume collects poems from 1981–1982. Many of these poems are not easily available to readers of Mullen's work. The second section brings together Mullen's poetry collections and fine art chapbooks: *Trimmings* (1991), *S*PeRM**K*T* (1992), *Muse & Drudge* (1995), *Sleeping with the Dictionary* (2002), *Broken Glish: Five Prose Poems* (2013) and *Urban Tumbleweed: Notes from a Tanka Diary* (2013). The third section brings together uncollected poems from 2001–2021. The uncollected poems have appeared in various print or virtual publications, but are mostly out of print or otherwise unavailable or difficult to access.

Her Silver-Tongued Companion begins in 1981 with Mullen's first book, *Tree Tall Woman* (Energy Earth Communications, 1981). *Tree Tall Woman* was first printed by Red River Women's Press, a feminist collective in Austin, Texas, whose members included Alice Embree, JoAnn Mulert, Rita Starpattern, and others. They agreed to publish Mullen's collection despite their initial objection to Mullen's poem, 'Miss Persephone', which had been provoked by Susan Brownmiller's *Against Our Will*, particularly her remarks about Emmett Till, which Angela Davis admonished in *Women, Race and Class* and Ishmael Reed satirised in his novel *Reckless Eyeballing*.[18] In August 1955, Carolyn Bryant, a twenty-one-year-old white woman, accused Emmett Till, a fourteen-year-old black boy, of making an unwelcome advance to her at a family store in Money, Mississippi. Those accusations led to the abduction and the brutal killing of Emmett Till. Carolyn Bryant, the white woman whose testimony helped acquit Till's murderers, later recanted her story. Gwendolyn Brooks wrote two poems in response to the case, and Toni Morrison wrote a play, *Dreaming Emmett* (1986). 'Miss Persephone', Mullen's response to Brownmiller's unfortunate comment on the Emmett Till case, was eventually included in *Tree Tall Women*, despite the misgivings of the printer collective, after Mullen explained the historical background of lynch mobs accusing black men of raping white women.

7

Miss Persephone

Persephone, you were one of those girls
who give rape a bad name.
A cherry ripe teenager,
attracted to the gangster type,
you let yourself into the bedroom
of that dark horny stranger from the underworld
He never had to lure you with candy
You were ready, randy.
And you sneaked away from home that night
to bed down with this sexy black devil.

But when your mother caught you,
you cried, "Rape!"
You batted your eyelashes innocently,
like a Hollywood belle.
"The dirty old black thing," you said,
"Trying to corrupt me."
You even claimed technical virginity,
"I only swallowed his seeds."

So now you lead a double life,
you two-faced hussy.
In spring you do the fake virgin act
to please your ma, who pretends to believe it.
But in the dark cold months of winter,
You heat the sheets of Hades
when your lusty lover
takes his share.

Shockley remarks that *Tree Tall Woman* is 'a collection of lyric poems largely in a southern, black vernacular voice, describing the speaker's family and community, their lives, her relationships with them, and the way this (black) cultural context shaped her sense of self'. Drawing on an interview with Mullen, Shockley observes: 'Mullen has credited the Black Arts Movement's racially politicised aesthetics with empowering her to treat her family and black culture more generally as poetic subjects.'[19] The print run of *Tree Tall Woman* narrowly escaped destruction in the 1981 Shoal

Creek flood, when water rose nearly to the top of a table where copies, fresh off the press, had been stacked, awaiting delivery. Austin's feminist bookstore, The Common Woman (now BookWoman), was among the first to stock Mullen's first poetry collection. African American bookstores also carried it, from Marcus Books in Oakland, California, to Hue-Man Experience in Denver, Colorado, and Shrine of the Black Madonna Cultural Center and Bookstore in Atlanta, Georgia. Lorenzo Thomas' quote on the back cover points to Mullen's engagement with folklore alongside Mullen's own conceptions: '. . . by far the most impressive of the younger black writers in Texas . . . Mullen's poetic recording of folklore also includes her own carefully intelligent interpretations.'

After graduation from University of Texas, Mullen worked at Austin Community College and in the Artists in Schools programme with poets Rosemary Catacalos, Naomi Shihab, Chuck Taylor, Lorenzo Thomas, and Evangelina Vigil. While writing *Tree Tall Woman* she lived and worked in different Texas cities: Austin, Houston, and Galveston, where Bob Ezra shot the photograph of a palm tree for the cover design. Mullen's poetry during this period was supported with readings sponsored by Austin-based organizations Texas Circuit, directed by Susan Bright, and Women & their Work, led by a group including Rita Starpattern, Deanna Stevenson, and Millie Wilson. Writers Shelby Hearon, Beverly Lowry, and Sherry Kafka Wagner nominated Mullen to the Texas Institute of Letters in 1982, and she served on the literature panel of the Texas Commission on the Arts 1982 to 1984.

Mullen's first book tour, with *Tree Tall Woman*, took her to Albuquerque and Santa Fe, New Mexico, for readings sponsored by a local NAACP branch, and at La Clínica de la Gente with poets including Joy Harjo, Simon Ortiz, and Cecilio García-Camarillo, editor of the journal *Caracol* and Mano Izquierda Books. The book tour extended as far as Los Angeles, where Mullen read at the Watts Towers Arts Center, and the San Francisco Bay Area, where Ishmael Reed organized a 'Downhome Poetry Reading' at the Unitarian Universalist Church of Berkeley. In addition to reading at local bookshops, coffeehouses, schools, and community centres, Mullen travelled to Louisiana, Mississippi, and Georgia for readings and conferences at historically black Dillard University, Tougaloo College, Jackson State University, and Spelman College, events associated with BLKARTSOUTH and the Southern Black Cultural Alliance, and readings organised by Tom Dent, Charles Rowell, and Jerry Ward, founding editors of the literary journal *Callaloo*.

Mullen's 1991 collection, *Trimmings*, placed the poet's writing in a lineage of prose poetry by Gertrude Stein in *Tender Buttons* and poetic prose in *Maud Martha* by Gwendolyn Brooks, and Jean Toomer's *Cane*. This was the period in which Mullen met Lee Ann Brown in New York, at the old Ear Inn on Spring Street, a serviceable bar in the historic home of James Brown, an African American hero of the Revolutionary War. Lee Ann Brown had heard about Mullen's work from Roberto Bedoya, who had invited Mullen to read at Intersection for the Arts in San Francisco's Mission District. Lee Ann Brown had recently founded Tender Buttons Press and published *Trimmings* following Bernadette Mayer's *Sonnets* and Anne Waldman's *Not a Male Pseudonym*. Loughran O'Connor penned an evocative drawing for the original cover of *Trimmings*. Gwendolyn Brooks described Mullen's work as 'short but pictureful poems with their own special music'. Bernadette Mayer too perceived the musical quality of Mullen's works, articulating the poems as: 'The loveliest melodious variations made guilelessly of the mention of the objects tender ... the things who became the same as the buttons with which we fasten together our wearings.' Charles Bernstein remarked on Mullen's 'poetics of cultural markers, the rhythms that make us us, new beats in a promenade of innovating charms'.

In 1991 Gil Ott scheduled Mullen to read at the Painted Bride Art Center in Philadelphia. About six people were in the audience, including the poet Major Jackson, who was also on the staff. Gil offered to publish *S*PeRM**K*T*, then in manuscript, with black-and-white photographs that he shot at his local supermarket. Following *Trimmings*, Mullen's response to the 'Objects' section of *Tender Buttons*, her next work responded to Stein's variations on 'Food' with Mullen's riffing on a supermarket shopping list. Mullen's collection proved highly successful. *S*PeRM**K*T* was the first book from Singing Horse Press that financially 'broke even', instead of leaving a negative balance.

Ott quickly and eagerly accepted Mullen's next work for publication, *Muse & Drudge*, a collection written partly to overcome what Mullen has termed 'aesthetic apartheid' – the social segregation of authors and audiences, presumed to be incompatible, divided by their respective cultural traditions and artistic tastes. Mullen recalls that the work began with her feeling that fragments of Sappho's ancient Greek poetry (translated by Diane Rayor) sound like a woman singing the blues. Alluding to singers from Sappho to Bessie Smith to rap performers, *Muse & Drudge* draws on traditions of lyric poetry, gospel, blues, folk, jazz, soul, and hip hop, artistic creations to which women contribute inspiration and perspiration. Mullen collaborated with Ott on the book design, using a photograph that Ott's friend Harvey Finkle had taken of an unknown black woman attending a public hearing to advocate for disability access. Mullen's friend, the photographer Judy Natal, gave Mullen the idea to crop and enlarge the greyscale portrait on a black-and-white copy machine, with further alterations to suit the cover design. Now considered Mullen's most well-known collection, *Muse & Drudge* quickly became a landmark work of African American literature and innovative women's writing. *Muse & Drudge* is possibly the favourite of African American poets and others interested in the intersectionality of Mullen's work and its potential audiences. Henry Louis Gates hailed the work as 'a compelling contribution to contemporary African American literature'. In his 'Poet's Choice' column for *The Washington Post*, Robert Hass wrote: '[Mullen's quatrains] invent, play with language, play with ideas, make all the sounds a poet can discover. It's an exuberant performance.' Sandra Cisneros' reception of Mullen's work ushered in the poet's reputation as 'the Queen of Hip Hyperbole'. Cisneros stated of *Muse and Drudge*: 'Hip hyperbole, thy queen is Ms. Mullen. Word rules. Harryette hype hip-hops and bops the taut poetry trapeze. Makes me want to marimba. Makes me want to riff when I raff. To always write write.'

In the mid-1990s Mullen's work carved her out as an important activist feminist writer. In 1996 Mullen was invited to collaborate with a group of feminist writers, artists, and computer programmers to create an interactive art project, a virtual 'house' constructed with digital tools on collective 'home pages' of a website sponsored by the Contemporary Museum of Photography at the University of California, Riverside, and Armand Hammer Museum in Los Angeles. Organised by Amelia Jones, Patricia A. Morton, and others, the project was a revision or e-version of the original Womanhouse, a brick-and-mortar space for women artists in Los Angeles in the 1970s. Within the larger collaborative project exploring the 'politics of domesticity', Mullen partnered with artist Yong Soon Min to design a conceptual piece, 'Porch', inspired partly by the 'Rooms' section of Gertrude Stein's three-part *Tender Buttons*. One of several texts Mullen composed for this project, 'Mantra for a Classless Society, or Mr. Roget's Neighborhood', is collected in *Sleeping with the Dictionary*, reproduced here in this Critical Edition.[20] Two other poems from this digital project, 'It's Not About the Menu' and 'Liberation of Ms. Liberty' draw an analogy between the porch or threshold of the home and the U.S. border. One poem refers to menus for 'ethnic' restaurants frequently hung on doorknobs in residential neighborhoods; the other reverses tropes of welcome in 'The New Colossus', a sonnet by Emma Lazarus inscribed on the Statue of Liberty.

The poems collected in this Critical Edition situate Mullen's works in the chronological order in which they were composed. However, *Blues Baby*, whilst written in 1981–1982, was not published until 2002. In 2001, Cynthia Hogue expressed interest in producing a new edition of *Tree Tall Woman*. Mullen suggested reprinting it alongside uncollected poems she had written with the support of fellowships from 1981 to 1982, as a resident at the Dobie-Paisano Ranch south of Austin, and in a casita of the Helene Wurlitzer Foundation in Taos, New Mexico. Mullen had set those poems aside when she enrolled in graduate school at the University of California, Santa Cruz. The title of the unpublished manuscript, *Blues Baby*, became the title for the combined collections. Alison Saar's soulful Topsy, in Mullen's words, 'graces the cover with a flash of the spirit'. Afaa Michael Weaver received *Blues Baby* as a 'pure delight, a relentless honesty'. For Hogue, the collection enabled a new understanding of Mullen, who was by 2002 considered to be 'a major black avant-garde artist'. Hogue observed: 'The poems in this collection provide the foundational information to begin to understand Mullen's extraordinary growth as a poet.' In this Critical Edition *Blues Baby* takes its place at the beginning of Mullen's oeuvre to date.

In 2002, Mullen was wondering where to send her next manuscript, *Sleeping with the Dictionary*. Cal Bedient encouraged Mullen to submit it to University of California Press where, with Robert Hass, Brenda Hillman, and Forrest Gander, he edited the New California Poetry series. Enrique Chagoya allowed the press to use his drawing *Line Essence Color* for the cover. *Sleeping with the Dictionary* was selected as a finalist for the National Book Award for Poetry in 2002 and *The Los Angeles Times* Book Prize for Poetry. Today *Sleeping with the Dictionary* is the most renowned of Mullen's works and the one that has received the most mainstream attention. *Sleeping with the Dictionary* has sold more copies, is in more libraries worldwide, is more often selected for anthologies, and received recognition from more national awards committees than the original *Muse & Drudge* and *Recyclopedia* (where *Muse & Drudge* is reprinted). Poems from *Sleeping with the Dictionary* were circulated widely during the 'racial reckoning' following the police murder of George Floyd, and have frequently been chosen for performance by high school students and community groups.

In 2006, Claudia Rankine recommended Mullen to Jeff Shotts at Graywolf Press, which then published *Recyclopedia*, a work combining three collections, *Trimmings*,

S*PeRM**K*T, and *Muse & Drudge*. The cover for *Recyclopedia* featured one of Mullen's most loved designs by the multimedia artist David Hammons, *Untitled (Night Train)*. *Recyclopedia* was honoured with a Beyond Margins Award from PEN. In 2006 NewTown Foundation of Los Angeles and Pasadena recruited and paired six animators with six 'spoken word' artists to collaborate in making new works. Thanks to Patricia Payne's determined effort, Mullen was among the participating writers. The resulting pieces were shown in a premiere screening, *Speak/See*, at the Wells Fargo Auditorium of the Autry Heritage Center. Featuring Mullen's performance of the title poem, *Waving the Flag*, a digital video collaboration with animation artist Sheila M. Sofian and musician William O. Darity was subsequently screened at local, national, and international festivals, winning a number of awards and citations. It was a PBS Independent Lens Online Shorts Festival Winner in 2007. Besides 'Waving the Flag', previously uncollected poems include others composed for special projects or in response to particular events. 'It's Not about the Menu' and 'Liberation of Ms. Liberty' were part of a collaboration with Yong Soon Min for *WomEnhouse*. 'The Fire This Time' was inspired by a malfunctioning fire alarm during a week at a Cave Canem poets' retreat on the grounds of the Cranbrook School, outside Detroit, Michigan. 'Remove Offensive Language' (a dictionary definition of the word 'bleep') was written for a poet trading card published by Fact-Simile. "I Want to Thank You, Betye Saar" was written for the artist's birthday.

The year 2013 saw the publication of a new work by Mullen, *Broken Glish*, a series of five prose poems collected in this edition and published here to a wide audience for the first time. In 2013 Sharon Dolin requested that Mullen judge the annual poetry chapbook contest sponsored by the Center for Book Arts in Manhattan. Along with works by the contest winner and two others in second and third place, the centre published *Broken Glish*, in a limited edition designed and letter-pressed with colourful monoprints by Delphi Basilicato. Mullen arrived early to sign copies of her book before reading with the other poets at the centre. Mullen dedicated the chapbook to Nicolás Guillén, Nancy Morejón, Pablo Neruda, and Alejandra Pizarnik, whose poetry inspired the work. *Urban Tumbleweed: Notes from a Tanka Diary* was also published in 2013 by Graywolf Press. Mullen's remarkable experiments with the tanka form brought her work to a new phase of avant-garde writing. Mullen's interest in Japanese poetry began when she attended a reading by Nanao Sakaki in Taos, New Mexico, during a six-month residency with the Wurlitzer Foundation. Later, as a visiting writer at Naropa University, Mullen found haiku and tanka collections in local bookstores of Boulder, Colorado, including one with translations by Robert Hass. They led Mullen to the library to check out classical poetry from anthologies commissioned by Japanese emperors. She started her tanka diary, prompted by a desire to walk and write daily, recording everyday encounters with 'nature' – however mediated and transformed by human habitation. She had been more attentive to the human/nature interface since Camille T. Dungy selected her poem 'European Folktale Variant' (from *Sleeping with the Dictionary*) for her anthology *Black Nature: Four Centuries of African American Nature Poetry*, reimagining what a 'nature poem' might be. Various interests and influences converge in *Urban Tumbleweed*. Mullen's American verses exist apart from Japanese literary tradition, although a few are directly inspired by translations of specific poems, such as Yosano Akiko's tanka about tangled hair, comparing it, in Mullen's case, to a curly cirrus cloud. Mullen found David Schalliol's photograph with an internet browser search for 'urban tumbleweed', and he kindly agreed to allow its use in Kyle G. Hunter's design for the cover. David Ulin reviewed it for *The Los Angeles Times*, and selected *Urban Tumbleweed* as a 'top book for fall'. Ulin remarked: 'Mullen is a walker, and in many ways, this is a walker's diary, a record of her interactions with the city at the level of the streets. But even more, it is a portrait of her mind in the act of reflection, sharply observed and deeply felt.' Mullen participated in a group reading in Stockholm on World Poetry Day, on

Mullen participated in a group reading in Stockholm on World Poetry Day, 21 March in 2011. As the picture documents, Mullen had pages of her work-in-progress, with John Swedenmark's translations, projected on a screen behind her. John Swedenmark, who translated part of *Urban Tumbleweed into Swedish*, took the photo.

21 March, 2011 (see Figure 1). That visit to Sweden resulted in a group of poems about walking on Stockholm's streets, collected in *Urban Tumbleweed*, along with tanka verses set primarily in California. Mullen's itinerary included taking a commuter train to a nearby university where she read and discussed her work with students and faculty members, gathering in cafes and restaurants with fellow poets, and wandering Stockholm's streets observing everyday wonders, such as a billboard advertising an obsolete brand of toothpaste. That is the origin of the tanka on a visual pun: 'tomato in the toothpaste'. (After writing it Mullen learned of homemade concoctions mixing the two things.) On her return from Sweden, Mullen created a limited-edition multimedia series, 'True Grit from Stockholm Streets', incorporating her original tanka verses along with gravel, dirt, snow, and assorted papers collected while wandering in the city (several Stockholm movie

theaters featured Joel and Ethan Coen's 2010 remake of the 1969 American western film adapted from Charles Portis' 1968 novel *True Grit*).

Mullen's most recent collection, *Open Leaves / poems from earth*, was published by Black Sunflowers Poetry Press in Summer 2023. Amanda Holiday, visual artist, poet, editor, and founder of Black Sunflowers, reached out from the UK, inviting Mullen to submit a manuscript for a chapbook series pairing poets with visual artists. Since *Urban Tumbleweed* and Mullen's contribution to *Renga for Obama*, edited by Major Jackson, Mullen had been composing occasional haiku, sent as greetings to friends and family. Mullen collected them and wrote dozens more. When Holiday suggested that Mullen include an epilogue, an extra 'gobstopper' in her bag of treats 'for good measure' (what people from Louisiana call *lagniappe*), Mullen added passages of prose. Holiday introduced Mullen to the art of Tiffanie Delune, whose paintings are reproduced in *Open Leaves*.

Critical Frames

Her Silver-Tongued Companion brings together five scholars of Mullen's work to address the key themes of African American feminism, vernacular innovation, bi-translation, improvisation, jazz, collaborative poetics, the lyric, food studies, the everyday, and the poetic forms of Tanka and Haiku. In doing so, the essays place Mullen among her key influences and contemporaries from Sappho to Adrienne Rich and Claudia Rankine. The essays convened for this companion open out both established strands of critical enquiry in relation to Mullen's work, and, vitally, offer new directions of critical thinking around Mullen's writing. Though distinct in their critical approaches, each essay pivots on Mullen's avant-garde writing practice.

Alan Gilbert opens the critical readings of Mullen's work with a 2006 essay spanning Mullen's early and later works, beginning with *Blues Baby*, and reaching to *Trimmings*,

S*PeRM**K*T, and *Muse & Drudge*, paying particular attention to *Sleeping with the Dictionary*. Gilbert examines the substantial changes in Mullen's work while at the same time arguing less for an evolution in Mullen's poetry and more for its varying ways of addressing core issues relating to self, identity, and community, specifically from Mullen's perspectives and experiences as a black woman. In an enlightening analysis of Mullen's publishing history, Gilbert argues that in republishing the earlier poems of *Blues Baby* around the same time as the newer work contained in *Sleeping with the Dictionary*, Mullen provides readers with a wide range of poetic styles and approaches to representations of black selves and communities. In turn, Gilbert contends, these representations are creative and critical responses to the ongoing ideological, social, and economic oppression of black people within the United States.

Emily Greenwood approaches Mullen's work from a classicist perspective, for the first time. Greenwood considers the ways in which Mullen, in her 1995 collection *Muse & Drudge*, reimagines the classical figure of the muse from the perspective of the othering of the black woman artist. In this work, Greenwood observes, Mullen explores the condition of being un-mused or a-mused, bracketed off within an aesthetic tradition of which one is manifestly a part – the muse mistaken for drudge or mule. At the heart of Mullen's collection, Greenwood argues, is the paradox of recognising oneself unimagined and of writing up from under prevailing stereotypes. Greenwood claims that by interweaving classical tropes and fragments into a creative dialogue which is characterised by the presence of several simultaneous discourses and intersecting identities, Mullen poses insistent questions about adaptation and proprietary use that reflect long-running debates about the interdependence of the aesthetic and the social in black poetics: who gets to traffic with the classics and on what terms? In this essay Greenwood analyses Mullen's 'bi-translation' of the Greek poet Sappho as Sapphire in the context of Mullen's experimental practice of working across and between multiple traditions and literatures, from highbrow to vernacular, replete with neoteric innovation and blues and jazz improvisation, offering a unique perspective on one of Mullen's most well-known works.

Solveig Daugaard probes the key issues surrounding the readership of Mullen's work, which the poet explores in her own critical work, and with which this Introduction opened. Daugaard's essay engages with Mullen's 1995 poem *Muse & Drudge*, taking up that which Mullen describes as the aesthetic apartheid she experienced as a black woman entering the American experimental poetry scene. In *Muse & Drudge*, Mullen produces a multivocal poetic texture drawing on multiple sources including classical, modernist, and Black Arts literature, media cultural motifs, and folk cultural forms – from quilting and graffiti to the dozens and the blues. Hereby, Daugaard argues, Mullen exposes the exclusion based on racial categories active in the poetic avant-garde and promotes a collective readership that breaks from the ideal of the reader as an independent and solitary figure considered neutral in terms of gender, race, and cultural background. Featuring forms not foremost perceived through the lens of individualised authorship alongside poetic interrogations of canonised authors such as Gertrude Stein, Daugaard claims that Mullen's poem also questions fundamental functionalities of print poetry attached to the concept of the self-sufficient author as tied to an implicitly white, Western modernity to push for the possibility of a more collaborative poetics. Also, through interventions into the book's design, including its cover, and the way metadata is presented, the stability of the individual author as an isolated figure is challenged. In this way, Daugaard understands the work as extending its zone of experimentation beyond the page to include the infrastructural conditions of production, distribution, and reading of literature that poetic canonisation has relied on for centuries.

Ayesha Ramachandran offers new critical avenues into Mullen's work from the perspective of early modern literature. Ramachandran enquires into Mullen's reimagining of a long lyric tradition reaching back to Callimachus and Sappho through intertextual patterns, Oulipian games, and allusive, phonic play in two of her collections, *Muse & Drudge* and *Sleeping with the Dictionary*. Anchored in Mullen's rewritings of Shakespeare, in her punning authorial signatures, in her riffs on 'Sonnet 130', and in her echoes of *A Midsummer Night's Dream*, Ramachandran's essay shows how Mullen's careful poetic engagement with formal and thematic elements of Shakespeare's verse transforms her versions of his writing into a series of sharp political reflections on the place of black women in the lyric tradition, as addressees, consumers, co-producers, and poets. By highlighting the similarity between Mullen's practice and early modern poetics, Ramachandran suggests ways in which Mullen's poetry is sharply anti-Romantic and anti-Adornian; arguing that Mullen's own often-stated interest in lyric traditions thus becomes an invitation to consider the entanglements between lyric histories and contemporary poetry.

Daniel Kane's essay brings the collection of essays full circle, through a study of Mullen's form. Readers familiar with Mullen's oeuvre and aware of Mullen's self-conscious manipulation of her publications to anticipate, integrate, and shape distinct audiences can understand her 2013 book *Urban Tumbleweed: Notes from a Tanka Diary* as engaged in conversation with Mullen's earlier works, Kane argues. For example, the visual appearance of *Urban Tumbleweed*, three discrete three-line tankas on each page, Kane claims, points back to Mullen's *Muse & Drudge*, in which four quatrains fill each page, thus inviting the reader to make connections across the texts. The fact that *Urban Tumbleweed* adapts a prescribed form also suggests Mullen's experiments with restraint-based forms in *Sleeping with the Dictionary*. *Urban Tumbleweed* is an important extension of Mullen's play with her audiences' expectations of how poetry produced by African American writers can and should reveal itself at the level of diction and form. And yet, as Kane's essay argues, there is much that is entirely new in *Urban Tumbleweed*, both in terms of what it brings into Mullen's project – a relatively straightforward urban pastoral mode, an adaptation of an ancient poetic form – and what it leaves out. Refusing to fetishise racial identity through the enactment of and play with dialect, Kane maintains, *Urban Tumbleweed* stands as perhaps Mullen's most challenging book yet in terms of confronting readers not just about their potential 'assumptions that "green" is white and "urban" is black' but, going further, their assumptions about what constitutes black voice itself as it is mediated through text.

The critical frames of the essays yield insight into the sheer dexterity of Harryette Mullen's poetry and her devotion to formal innovation. As Claudia Rankine remarks, Mullen 'is our most underrecognized major poet'. It is the aim of this volume to provide a thorough assemblage of Mullen's avant-garde works that reveals the importance of her work to the landscape of contemporary poetry.

Notes

1. Al Filreis made this comment on PoemTalk, the podcast series at Kelly Writers House, on the episode, 'Trance of Language: A Discussion of 'Sleeping with the Dictionary' and 'Dim Lady' from *Sleeping with the Dictionary*', featuring Maxe Crandall, Larissa Lai, and Julia Bloch. https://www.poetryfoundation.org/podcasts/158026/trance-of-language
2. Claudia Rankine, 'Claudia Rankine Wishes More Writers Thought About Whiteness', *By the Book* series, *The New York Times*, 1 December 2020. https://www.nytimes.com/2020/11/26/books/review/claudia-rankine-by-the-book-interview.html?action=click&module=Well&pgtype=Homepage&section=Books
3. Harryette Mullen, 'Imagining the Unimagined Reader: Writing to the Unborn and Including the Excluded', in *The Cracks Between What We are and What We are Supposed to Be* (Tuscaloosa: University of Alabama Press, 2012), pp. 3–9.
4. Mullen, 'Imagining the Unimagined Reader', p. 8.
5. Mullen, 'Imagining the Unimagined Reader', p. 4.
6. Mullen, 'Imagining the Unimagined Reader', p. 8.
7. Hank Lazer, 'Introduction', in Harryette Mullen, *The Cracks Between What We Are and What We are Supposed To Be*.

8. Lazer, 'Introduction'.
9. Harryette Mullen, 'Poetry and Identity', in *The Cracks Between What We Are and What We are Supposed To Be*.
10. Mullen, 'Poetry and Identity', p. 10.
11. Mullen, 'Poetry and Identity', p. 10.
12. Evie Shockley, *Renegade Poetics: Black Aesthetics and Formal Innovation in African American Poetry* (Iowa City: University of Iowa Press, 2011), p. 10.
13. Shockley, *Renegade Poetics*, p. 18.
14. Anthony Reed, *Freedom Time: The Poetics and Politics of Black Experimental Writing* (Baltimore, MD: Johns Hopkins University Press), p. 23.
15. Reed, *Freedom Time*, p. 141.
16. Reed, *Freedom Time*, p. 149.
17. Harryette Mullen, 'Poetry and Identity', 12.
18. In *Against Our Will: Men Women and Rape*, first published in 1975, Susan Brownmiller claims: 'Emmett Till was going to show his black buddies that he, and by inference they, could get a white woman and Carolyn Bryant was the nearest convenient object. In concrete terms, the accessibility of all white women was on review.' In another part of the book Brownmiller expands: 'It took fifteen years for me to resolve these questions in my own mind, and to understand the insult implicit in Emmett Till's whistle, the depersonalised challenge of "I can have you" with or without the racial aspect.' Despite the widespread outcry to Brownmiller's racist comments, the book continued to circulate unmodified.
19. Shockley, *Renegade Poetics*, p. 83.
20. Although *WomEnhouse* eventually was taken down, Pat Morton's essay, 'A Visit to WomEnhouse' appears in *Architecture of the Everyday*, edited by Deborah Berke and Steven Harris (Princeton Architectural Press/Yale Publications on Architecture, 1997).

Her Silver-Tongued Companion

Harryette Mullen

I

Collected Poems
1981–1982

Blues Baby: Early Poems
(1981–1982)

Of Two Minds

An eye opens, a door closes
a flower shatters

A plot requires opposing forces
"half shameful love"

Balance, not ambivalence
Like my back ain't got no bone

Swaying or wavering as if losing
or gaining—momentum, inertia

A door ajar, container
the thing contained

Ambivalence
a word coined by Freud

A wasp waist, an hourglass figure
The hand is quicker

He cuts quite a figure
A body bisected

A proportion of parts
pleasing to whose eye

Balance as cancellation

How to account for blood in a shoe
A tight shoe, a tight fit

Daily mutilations, small sad prayers
To enter, to be entered

To open, perhaps for the last time
Moving toward and then away

Balance, which multiplies force
That which remains

A Woman is Dreaming

A woman who cringes at the stiffness of starched petticoats
has climbed into an alligator briefcase
with teeth that snap shut on crisp quarterly reports.
All night she dreams of lace,
frothy and white as a splash of fresh cream.

A woman shocked at lotus feet
folded in on themselves like paper fans
is zippered up in leather boots.
Her dreams are blue-satin slippers
embroidered with silver threads.

A woman who wears aluminum skin
is dreaming herself soft as a rabbit's pelt.

A woman whose hands are tiny bird claws
invents a pair of hands in her sleep.
The hands in her dreams are capable and large:
strong brown hands with soft pink palms.

A woman dying slowly in a rotting bathrobe
sees a red gingham dress skipping rope in a dream.

A shy blind girl with eyes like wilted flowers
is dreaming the image of pink,
the hue of rosebuds.
A hungry woman sleeping on her empty stomach
dreams she is pregnant.
She gives birth to a loaf of bread.

Cartoon Men

glided in inked-in tuxedos
blew smoke rings impeccably
left oblique shadows
with the hat-check girl
They could tiptoe on thin air
or shin up a beam of light
          The music was mad
They jitterbugged out of sight

You Who Walked Through the Fire

You who walked through the fire
and lived to laugh at our invented fevers,
your lives are blueprints for courage,
yet you inoculated us with fear—
sent us out with terrors sewn into our pockets.

Having reserved all bravery for yourselves,
you wonder how you spawned such weaklings.
You look at us, amazed at what you have made,
doubting that our narrow bodies are worth
the whirlwinds that carved us out of your solid lives.

What might I have accomplished with all my spendthrift
freedom added to your inheritance of faith?
What miracles that I'm afraid to try
with only the strength of my two hands?

She Landed on the Moon

She'd studied the science of motion,
applied physics to the wound
and her loneliness healed.

She landed on the moon,
alert in the snarl of machinery,
shining in complex uniform
with zippers and pockets
for emergency secrets,
a helmet to protect her head.

Earphones played a musical wind
where not a tree was blowing.
Computers drove her there,
calculating her fall.

She landed on a soft spot on the moon,
evading the stony heart.

Emerging into braver solitude,
she walked with new gravity,
her music parting the slow silence.

II

Poetry Collections
1991–2013

Sleeping with the Dictionary
(2002)

All She Wrote

Forgive me, I'm no good at this. I can't write back. I never read your letter. I can't say I got your note. I haven't had the strength to open the envelope. The mail stacks up by the door. Your hand's illegible. Your postcards were defaced. "Wash your wet hair"? Any document you meant to send has yet to reach me. The untied parcel service never delivered. I regret to say I'm unable to reply to your unexpressed desires. I didn't get the book you sent. By the way, my computer was stolen. Now I'm unable to process words. I suffer from aphasia. I've just returned from Kenya and Korea. Didn't you get a card from me yet? What can I tell you? I forgot what I was going to say. I still can't find a pen that works and then I broke my pencil. You know how scarce paper is these days. I admit I haven't been recycling. I never have time to read the *Times*. I'm out of shopping bags to put the old news in. I didn't get to the market. I meant to clip the coupons. I haven't read the mail yet. I can't get out the door to work, so I called in sick. I went to bed with writer's cramp. If I couldn't get back to writing, I thought I'd catch up on my reading. Then *Oprah* came on with a fabulous author plugging her best-selling book.

The Anthropic Principle

The pope of cosmology addresses a convention. When he talks the whole atmosphere changes. He speaks through a computer. When he asks can you hear me, the whole audience says yes. It's a science locked up in a philosophical debate. There are a few different theories. There could be many different realities. You might say ours exists because we do. You could take a few pounds of matter, heat it to an ungodly temperature, or the universe was a freak accident. There may be a limit to our arrogance, but one day the laws of physics will read like a detailed instruction manual. A plane that took off from its hub in my hometown just crashed in the President's hometown. The news anchor says the pilot is among the dead. I was hoping for news of the President's foreign affair with a diplomat's wife. I felt a mystical connection to the number of confirmed dead whose names were not released. Like the time I was three handshakes from the President. Like when I thought I heard that humanitarians dropped a smart blond on the Chinese embassy. Like when the cable was severed and chairs fell from the sky because the pilot flew with rusty maps. What sane pilot would land in that severe rain with hard hail and gale-force wind. With no signal of distress. With no fog-horns to warn the civilians, the pilot lost our moral compass in the bloody quagmire of collateral damage. One theory says it's just a freak accident locked up in a philosophical debate. It's like playing poker and all the cards are wild. Like the arcane analysis of a black box full of insinuations of error.

Any Lit

You are a ukulele beyond my microphone
You are a Yukon beyond my Micronesia
You are a union beyond my meiosis
You are a unicycle beyond my migration
You are a universe beyond my mitochondria
You are a Eucharist beyond my Miles Davis
You are a euphony beyond my myocardiogram
You are a unicorn beyond my Minotaur
You are a eureka beyond my maitai
You are a Yuletide beyond my minesweeper
You are a euphemism beyond my myna bird
You are a unit beyond my mileage
You are a Yugoslavia beyond my mind's eye
You are a yoo-hoo beyond my minor key
You are a Euripides beyond my mime troupe
You are a Utah beyond my microcosm
You are a Uranus beyond my Miami
You are a youth beyond my mylar
You are a euphoria beyond my myalgia
You are a Ukrainian beyond my Maimonides
You are a Euclid beyond my miter box
You are a Univac beyond my minus sign
You are a Eurydice beyond my maestro
You are a eugenics beyond my Mayan
You are a U-boat beyond my mind control
You are a euthanasia beyond my miasma
You are a urethra beyond my Mysore
You are a Euterpe beyond my Mighty Sparrow
You are a ubiquity beyond my minority

You are a eunuch beyond my migraine
You are a Eurodollar beyond my miserliness
You are a urinal beyond my Midol
You are a uselessness beyond my myopia

Black Nikes

We need quarters like King Tut needed a boat. A slave could row him to heaven from his crypt in Egypt full of loot. We've lived quietly among the stars, knowing money isn't what matters. We only bring enough to tip the shuttle driver when we hitch a ride aboard a trailblazer of light. This comet could scour the planet. Make it sparkle like a fresh toilet swirling with blue. Or only come close enough to brush a few lost souls. Time is rotting as our bodies wait for now I lay me down to earth. Noiseless patient spiders paid with dirt when what we want is stardust. If nature abhors an expensive appliance, why does the planet suck ozone? This is a big-ticket item, a thickety ride. Please page our home and visit our sigh on the wide world's ebb. Just point and cluck at our new persuasion shoes. We're opening the gate that opens our containers for recycling. Time to throw down and take off on our launch. This flight will nail our proof of pudding. The thrill of victory is, we're exiting earth. We're leaving all this dirt.

Bleeding Hearts

Crenshaw is a juicy melon. Don't spit, and when you're finished, wash your neck. Tonight we lead with bleeding hearts, sliced raw or scooped with a spoon. I'll show my shank. I'd rend your cares with my shears. If I can't scare cash from the ashen crew, this monkey wrench has scratch to back my business. This ramshackle stack of shotguns I'm holding in my scope. I'm beady-eyed as a bug. Slippery as a sardine. Salty as a kipper. You could rehash me for breakfast. Find my shrinking awe, or share your wink. I'll get a rash wench. We'll crash a shower of cranes. I'm making bird seed to stick in a hen's craw. Where I live's a wren shack. Pull back. Show wreck. Black fade.

Coals to Newcastle, Panama Hats from Ecuador

Watching television in Los Angeles. This scene performed in real time. In real life, a pretty picture walking and sitting still. It's still life with fried spam, lite poundcake, nondairy creme. It's death by chocolate. It's corporate warfare as we know it. I'm stuck on the fourth step. There's no statue or stature of limitations. I'll be emotionally disturbed for as long as it takes. You can give a man a rock or you can teach him to rock. Access your higher power. Fax back the map of your spiritual path. Take twenty drops tincture of worry wort. Who's paying for this if you're not covered? You're too simple to be so difficult. Malicious postmodernism. Petroleum jelly donut dunked in elbow grease. You look better going than coming. You look like death eating microwave popcorn. Now that I live alone, I'm much less introspective. Now you sound more like yourself.

Daisy Pearl

More than a woman's name. Her traditional shape. Rapidly spread and rubbed with a wedge. Straight drunk with a crooked lick. A brief suck on time. Diminutive. Promptly popular still on the border. As one version of stamina went. A great show of suffering in order to arouse. There were sweet ones. Frozen ones and fruity ones. Her little resemblance to the original. Shake her one key part. Control her ice. Shake her poor stem. Her rim rubbed. Slice juice and pour control out with dusty salt. Or to taste if desired.

Denigration

Did we surprise our teachers who had niggling doubts about the picayune brains of small black children who reminded them of clean pickaninnies on a box of laundry soap? How muddy is the Mississippi compared to the third-longest river of the darkest continent? In the land of the Ibo, the Hausa, and the Yoruba, what is the price per barrel of nigrescence? Though slaves, who were wealth, survived on niggardly provisions, should inheritors of wealth fault the poor enigma for lacking a dictionary? Does the mayor demand a recount of every bullet or does city hall simply neglect the black alderman's district? If I disagree with your beliefs, do you chalk it up to my negligible powers of discrimination, supposing I'm just trifling and not worth considering? Does my niggling concern with trivial matters negate my ability to negotiate in good faith? Though Maroons, who were unruly Africans, not loose horses or lazy sailors, were called renegades in Spanish, will I turn any blacker if I renege on this deal?

Dim Lady

My honeybunch's peepers are nothing like neon. Today's special at Red Lobster is redder than her kisser. If Liquid Paper is white, her racks are institutional beige. If her mop were Slinkys, dishwater Slinkys would grow on her noggin. I have seen table-cloths in Shakey's Pizza Parlors, red and white, but no such picnic colors do I see in her mug. And in some minty-fresh mouth-washes there is more sweetness than in the garlic breeze my main squeeze wheezes. I love to hear her rap, yet I'm aware that Muzak has a hipper beat. I don't know any Marilyn Monroes. My ball and chain is plain from head to toe. And yet, by gosh, my scrumptious Twinkie has as much sex appeal for me as any lanky model or platinum movie idol who's hyped beyond belief.

Ectopia

A stout bomb wrapped with a bow. With wear, you tear. It's true you sour or rust. Some of us were sure you're in a rut. We bore your somber rub and storm. You were true, but you rust. On our tour out, we tore, we two. You were to trust in us, and we in you. Terribly, you tear. You tear us. You tell us you're true. Are you sure? Most of you bow to the mob. Strut with worms, strew your woe. So store your tears, tout your worst. Be a brute, if you must. You tear us most terribly. To the tomb, we rue our rust and rot. You tear. You wear us out. You try your best, but we're bust. You tear out of us. We tear from stem to stem. You trouble, you butter me most. You tear, but you tell us, trust us to suture you.

Elliptical

They just can't seem to ... They should try harder to ... They ought to be more ... We all wish they weren't so ... They never ... They always ... Sometimes they ... Once in a while they ... However it is obvious that they ... Their overall tendency has been ... The consequences of which have been ... They don't appear to understand that ... If only they would make an effort to ... But we know how difficult it is for them to ... Many of them remain unaware of ... Some who should know better simply refuse to ... Of course, their perspective has been limited by ... On the other hand, they obviously feel entitled to ... Certainly we can't forget that they ... Nor can it be denied that they ... We know that this has had an enormous impact on their ... Nevertheless their behavior strikes us as ... Our interactions unfortunately have been ...

European Folk Tale Variant

for the archives of Toni Cade Bambara

The way the story goes, a trespassing towheaded pre-teen barged into the rustic country cottage of a nuclear family of anthropomorphic bruins. Her motivation? Who can be sure? Some say the youthful offender was an innocent maiden who lost her sense of direction in the lush growth of the virgin pine forest. Or perhaps the elders of her tribe had neglected to attend to her proper socialization. In any case, this flaxen-haired vixen perpetrated a "B and E," a felony punishable by law. The incorrigible pre-adolescent didn't stop with trespassing, or even with breaking and entering. The finicky home invader helped herself to generous portions of the ursine honey eaters' whole grain breakfast cereal, vandalized their heirloom antique furniture. Then, after tiring herself out with so much wanton destruction, the platinum blonde delinquent took a refreshing beauty nap in the bruin family's bedroom—just like she thought she was a guest at a cozy bed and breakfast inn. Returning from their fishing expedition, the family could barely express their shock and dismay, seeing the shambles the puerile hoodlum had made of their woodland homestead. Despite their emotional trauma, they successfully expelled the rude intruder from their charming bungalow. With the assistance of the neighborhood crime patrol, law enforcement officers were able to apprehend and incarcerate the callow miscreant, who has been sentenced to juvenile detention. Attorneys representing the Ursidae family interests have filed suit against the criminally negligent parents of the wayward youth, and expect that the bruins will be awarded a substantial sum for emotional distress as well as for extensive damage to their property.

Eurydice

Can't wait to be sprung from shadow,
to be known from a hole in the ground.
Scarcely silent though often unheard.
Winding, wound. Wounded wind.
She turned, and turns. She opens.
Keep the keys, that devil told her.
Guess the question. Dream the answer.
Tore down almost level.
A silence hardly likely.
Juicy voices. Pour them on.
Music sways her, she concedes,
as darker she goes deeper.

Exploring the Dark Content

This dream is not a map.
A poem is not the territory.

The dreamer reclines in a barbershop
carpeted with Afro turf.
In the dark some soul yells.

It hurts to walk barefoot
on cowrie shells.

Fancy Cortex
reading Jayne Cortez

I'm using my plain brain to imagine her fancy cortex. As if my lowly mollusk could wear so exalted a mantle as her pontifex pallium. As if the knots and tangles of my twisted psyche could mesh with her intricate synaptic network of condensed neural convolutions. As if my simple chalk could fossilize the memory of her monumental reefs of caulifloral coral. As if my shallow unschooled shoals could reckon the calculus of her konk's brainwave tsunami. As if the pedestrian software of my mundane explorer could map as rounded colonies the *terra incognita* of her undiscovered hemispheres. As if the speculative diagnosis of my imaging technology could chart the direction of her intuitive intellect. As if the inquisitive iris of my galaxy-orbiting telescope could see as far as her vision. As if the trained nostrils of my narco-bloodhound could sniff out what she senses in the wind. As if my duty-free bottle of jerk sauce could simulate the fire ant *picante* that inflames her tongue of rage. As if the gray matter of my dim bulb could be enlightened by the brilliance of her burning watts. As if her divergent universification might fancy the microcosm of my prosaic mind.

Free Radicals

She brought the radish for the horses, but not a bouquet for Mother's Day. She brought the salad to order with an unleavened joke. Let us dive in and turn up green in search of our roots. She sang the union maid with a lefty longshoreman. They all sang rusty freedom songs, once so many tongues were loosened. She went to bed sober as always, without a drop of wine. She was invited to judge a spectacle. They were a prickly pair in a restaurant of two-way mirrors with rooms for interrogation. The waiter who brought a flaming dessert turned the heat from bickering to banter. She braked for jerk chicken on her way to meet the patron saint of liposuction. His face was cut from the sunflower scene, as he was stuffing it with cheesecake. Meanwhile, she slurped her soup alone at the counter before the gig. Browsers can picture his uncensored bagel rolling around in cyberspace. His half-baked metaphor with her scrambled ego. They make examples of intellectuals who don't appreciate property. She can't just trash the family-style menu or order by icon. Now she's making *kimchee* for the museum that preserved her history in a jar of pickled pig feet. They'd fix her oral tradition or she'd trade her oral fixation. Geechees are rice eaters. It's good to get a rice cooker if you cook a lot of rice. Please steam these shellfish at your own risk. Your mother eats blue-green algae to rid the body of free radicals.

Kamasutra Sutra

This is a story I have heard:
Entwined in a passionate embrace
with his beloved wife,
the holy one exclaimed,
"I have reached enlightenment!"

His devoted partner responded,
"I'm truly happy for you, my love,
and if you can give me another minute,
I believe I'll get there too."

The Lunar Lutheran

In chapels of opals and spice, O Pisces pal, your social pep makes you a friend to all Episcopals. Brush off lint, gentile, but it's not intelligent to beshrew the faith of Hebrews. I heard this from a goy who taught yoga in the home of Goya. His Buddhist robe hid this budding D bust in this B movie dud. If Ryan bites a rep, a Presbyterian is best in prayer. Oh tears oxen trod! To catch oil, or a man born to the manor, you need a Catholic, Roman. On Mon. morn, Mom hums "Om" with no other man but Norm or Ron. A Mormon son would gladly leave a gas slave in Las Vegas for a hut in Utah. These slums I'm from, I'm leaving, Miss Lum, with a slim sum donated by some Muslims. What would it cost to gain the soul of an agnostic? Where the atheist is at, God only knows! 'Tis hate, he is at the heist. A Baptist was able to stab a pit bull when the sun hid behind some Hindus. To fan a mess, I write manifestos. So said the lunar Lutheran.

Music for Homemade Instruments
improvising with Douglas Ewart

I dug you artless, I dug you out. Did you re-do? You dug me less, art. You dug, let's do art. You dug me, less art. Did you re-do? If I left art out, you dug. My artless dug-out. You dug, let art out. Did you re-do, dug-out canoe? Easy as a porkpie piper-led cinch. Easy as a baby bounce. Hop on pot, tin pan man. Original abstract, did you re-do it? Betting on shy cargo, strutting dimpled low-cal strumpets employ a hipster to blow up the native Formica. Then divide efficiency on hairnets, flukes, faux saxons. You dug me out, didn't you? Did you re-do? Ever curtained to experiment with strumpet strutting. Now curtains to milk laboratory. Desecrated flukes & panics displayed by mute politicians all over this whirly-gig. Hey, you dug! Art lasts. Did you re-do? Well-known mocker of lurching unused brains, tribal & lustrous diddlysquats, Latin dimension crepe paper & muscular stacks. Curtains for perky strumpets strutting with mites in the twilight of their origami funkier purses. Artless, you dug. Did you re-do? For patting wood at flatland, thanks. For bamboozle flukes at Bama, my seedy medication. Thanks for my name in the yoohoo. Continental camp-out, percolating throughout the whirly-gig on faux saxon flukes. You dug art, didn't you? Did you re-do?

Naked Statues

Oscars for the war of noses. With a mummy out of Egypt, a prosthetic muppet. Opening shot: cliché of travel genre. In several scenes, a woman put together in black, white, or khaki. A woman with her back up like his map of mountain. Finally, she dies. Then, at last, he dies. So romantic are the patient English. This all went on when I was making up my syllabus. Telephone and radio told who the winners were. I didn't need a crystal. Last time I watched was leopard chair and whoopie cushion. That's when I saw the industry of light, our buttered roll. These are the friends of inklish, I was told, by someone from an anglophile race. They read all the great books and perform them in the garden of naked statues.

Natural Anguish

Every anguish is arbitrary but no one is neuter. Bulldozer can knock down dikes. Why a ragged bull don't demolish the big house? The fired cook was deranged. On the way back when I saw red I thought ouch. Soon when I think colored someone bleeds. The agency tapping my telephone heard my pen drop. Now I'm walking out of pink ink. We give microphones to the voiceless to amplify their silence. The complete musician could play any portion of the legacy of the instrument. My ebony's under the ocean. Please bring back my bone (sic) to me. Once was illegal for we to testify. Now all us do is testify. We's all prisoners of our own natural anguish. It's the rickety rickshaw that will drive us to the brink.

Once Ever After

There was this princess who wet the bed through many mattresses, she was so attuned. She neither conversed with magical beasts nor watched her mother turn into a stairwell or a stoop. Her lips were. Her hair was. Her complexion was. Her beauty or her just appearance. What she wore. She was born on a chessboard, with parents and siblings, all royal. Was there a witch? Was she enchanted, or drugged? When did she decide to sleep? Dreaming a knight in armor, she thought it meant jousting. His kind attack with streamers. A frog would croak. A heart would cough after only one bite. Something was red. There was wet and there was weather. She couldn't make it gold without his name. Her night shifts in the textile mill. She forgot she was a changeling peasant girl. Spinning, she got pricked. That's where roses fell and all but one fairy wept. It remains that she be buried alive, knowing that a kiss is smaller than a delayed hunger.

Present Tense

Now that my ears are connected to a random answer machine, the wrong brain keeps talking through my hat. Now that I've been licked all over by the English tongue, my common law spout is suing for divorce. Now that the Vatican has confessed and the White House has issued an apology, I can forgive everything and forget nothing. Now the overdrawn credits roll as the bankrupt star drives a patchwork cab to the finished line, where a broke robot waves a mended tablecloth, which is the stale flag of a checkmate career. Now that the history of civilization has been encrypted on a medium grain of rice, it's taken the starch out of the stuffed shorts. Now as the Voice of America crackles and fades, the market reports that today the Euro hit a new low. Now as the reel unravels, our story unwinds with the curious dynamic of an action flick without a white protagonist.

She Swam On from Sea to Shine

Hide and seek, where the tree decided to sleep was where she ran. She ran away with a ruckus. The baby girl was stolen by a tipsy woman came to take her. Where they found her in the mud. She'd stolen a doll. Her doll got sick, she died. The brown doll from her father. The pink doll came from somewhere else. She had drowsy eyes like marbles. The rabbit was painted on the furniture in the room with pom-pom curtains. The pig slept at her grandmother's. The pig that ate money, not the country pig that ate molasses and sunglasses. Where her mother kept a canoe and paddle. Where stiff lace stood, in the city not the country, where they fed their stinky sheep. Paper shell pecans, climb high. Sweet figs and green plums in forbidden backyards. She remembers sleeping on a train. She remembers a long sleep, rocking, rocking. She had her dress on all the way. Asleep, diving into dreams. Salty and warm, like ocean, like broth. Another time she slept, she dreamed of rats. When she woke up, the kittens were all killed. We're in a photograph with a handsome man smiling. Seersucker suits are what to wear in summer. That other man I don't remember, the one who made your hair fall. That's when the doctor said you need a root. You need your roots. You need a doctor who knows roots and will root for you. That's how we all got better. That's how we got to all your exes live in Texas. All the livelong day with the cowgirl you left behind.

Those saxophone streets and scratchy sidewalks. Those Baptist conventions. That steamy summer. The boy who threw tar on me. The boy who made me his tar baby. The one who broke my watch, knocked me down, pushed me over. The boy who threw rocks at me. The boy who lost his foot under the wheels of a train. The boy who bought me ice cream. The girl who was my friend. The girl who wanted to give me a kitten. The girl with burnt hands. The girl whose house was dark. The girl who never wore socks. The girl who said, "Poot on you." I had a ribbon in my hair. I was too proper and prissy. I must think I'm something. I must think she's nothing.

In the beginning, we stay with the preacher. We sit sweating on the mercy seat. We hear the preacher shout. We feel the fire in this man who built the church that burned down. This preacher who read Nietzsche. This preacher who was a carpenter with bent nails, who was the father of the cowgirl who ironed his handkerchiefs. The big man who cheered at wrestling matches, who drove a dark Chevy, who wore white shirts stiff from the laundry, who sang, "There was a crooked man, who had a crooked smile." She recalls a sixpence, a pig, a crooked little stile. He knew a stile could get them over. He knew a thing or two, and so did the lady who made crab cakes. The lady who fried scrapple. The lady with peach tree switches, who knew that a spigot was a faucet. Her *chaise longue*, her *porte-cochere*, her *chiffonier*. She didn't want the cowgirl to be a boll weevil. She wanted us where we were, not in the garage. She wanted us in the church where everyone shouted.

We started selling and counting. Anything from earthworms and bottles to paper shell pecans. She saved green stamps and we ate pinto beans from dented cans. She found a house with bramble bushes. We found a lovely alley made dizzy circles. We found a house with attic rooms. A magic chef in the kitchen and a genie to keep it clean. We kept moving until we moved the neighbors out. They ran to Runaway Bay. They hid at Hideway Lake. Those neighbors who were not neighborly, who didn't want us for neighbors.

63

The nuns were smart teachers, but she didn't care for them. They didn't care for her and called her friend a guttersnipe. The nuns in their brick *pan dulce* magnolia convent, their virgin rose *tortilla de maíz* garden grotto, their *Carnicería Chapultepec* chapel. These nuns don't talk Spanish, you could say French. Parlor fluent frenchy, jumble lying crawfish pie filling gumball. They taught girls to knit. They taught her to hit the piano. They taught all the girls to say hell merry fuller grays, dolores wit chew, blast duh art dower mung wimmen, blast dis fruit uh duh loom, cheez whiz. Anomie, dull party, dull filly, dull spitter shoo sanity. I am my mother's daughter who put me in the water to see if I could swim. My hair went back to Africa. I baptize thee. Hiccup, hiccup, hiccup.

High school was a bluster. She wasn't a bother. High school was a thick brick. She was knocked out. High school was too high, she was too low. High school was too low, she was too high. High school was too many schedules she crashed. Who could remember the combination. High school was hormones and hers were a moan, she wasn't a whore or a harmed one. No one was too harsh. High school was hot, she wasn't cool. She loved the books and not the boys. They moved too much, they blur. Too many books on her head, her leaky calendar. Too much gossip, her unlocked locker. Too much mother, she wouldn't hop. She wasn't a case of textbooks. Never that. She was a cartoon. She was a poem. Anyone would stutter trying to recite.

After perusing all the pamphlets, she went where she had been, where she knew how. It was a place she knew she could. So big no one would notice in a green location. She knew the uniforms, not the sunbathers. She kept her eye on the tower, rehearsed her sitting ducks. She believed the room was haunted, the furniture walked. Her friend had gone to a school where she misplaced her mind. She never found her friend again, her box of comprehension. There were new girls now, the ones who ironed tortillas and made beans drunk.

They knew that *sopa* isn't soap, *ropa* isn't rope, and butter is meant to kill ya.

If only she could play bid whist, if only she could tell someone. If only she had only eaten cassava, not listened to so much jazz. If only she had a gospel voice, not a notebook full of Babylon. If only she had obeyed her mother, if only she could disobey. If only she hadn't been to prison to visit the afflicted. If whiskey were water and I were a duck. If only if you only knew she wouldn't try to tell you.

She got that piece of paper and ran with it. Somewhere she'd found a tongue she used gingerly. She spoke up, she didn't lie down. If she did lie, she made it a big one. She spoke for a wagon wheel, she got the grease. They paid her to be smart, or dumb, it didn't matter. If they paid her, she could eat. If they didn't, she could go. She was always writing anyway, it didn't matter. She fell into a trance. That's how he took her with him where he went, and so she came along and there she was. When he wanted to bust her, she wasn't in shock, there was warning. Instead of bursting, she ran. She got used to running.

More paper, more pencils, more writing, she went every-where she could. She went on a whim, on a limb, she limped and whimpered. She slowed down, she settled, she got stuck. She came loose, she mended. She came undone, she repaired herself again. She shook her groove thing and got it on. She stepped on a pin, the pin bent. Good thing she got that tetanus shot. Time for a booster.

When the ship went down, she wouldn't sink, had to swim, she brought her suit. She'd float like a jellyfish, sting like a man of war, or seaweed ain't salty. Water was her element, she swam on. Right through a tsunami, she cut with scissor kicks. She caught a wave, she got in a flap, she was flippant. From sea, she ran past shark teeth. Like shine, see. If I'm lying, I'm flying. From sea to shine, she swam on. The whales sang Celtic music, dolphins frisked her. She was worked over and under she let her mind wander. Let it roll and keep on rolling on and on. Revolution is a cycle that never ends. Rumors of May made mermaids murmur. Plato opens utopia to poets on opiates.

Sleeping with the Dictionary

I beg to dicker with my silver-tongued companion, whose lips are ready to read my shining gloss. A versatile partner, conversant and well-versed in the verbal art, the dictionary is not averse to the solitary habits of the curiously wide-awake reader. In the dark night's insomnia, the book is a stimulating sedative, awakening my tired imagination to the hypnagogic trance of language. Retiring to the canopy of the bedroom, turning on the bedside light, taking the big dictionary to bed, clutching the unabridged bulk, heavy with the weight of all the meanings between these covers, smoothing the thin sheets, thick with accented syllables—all are exercises in the conscious regimen of dreamers, who toss words on their tongues while turning illuminated pages. To go through all these motions and procedures, groping in the dark for an alluring word, is the poet's nocturnal mission. Aroused by myriad possibilities, we try out the most perverse positions in the practice of our nightly act, the penetration of the denotative body of the work. Any exit from the logic of language might be an entry in a symptomatic dictionary. The alphabetical order of this ample block of knowledge might render a dense lexicon of lucid hallucinations. Beside the bed, a pad lies open to record the meandering of migratory words. In the rapid eye movement of the poet's night vision, this dictum can be decoded, like the secret acrostic of a lover's name.

Souvenir from Anywhere

People of color untie-dyed. Got nothing to lose but your CPT-shirts. You're all just a box of crayons. The whole ball of wax would make a lovely decorator candle on a Day of the Dead Santeria Petro Vodou altar. Or how about these yin-yang earrings to balance your energy? This rainbow crystal necklace, so good for unblocking your chi and opening the chakras? Hey, you broke it, you bought it! No checks accepted. Unattended children will be sold as slaves.

Suzuki Method

El Niño brought a typhoon of tom-toms from Tokyo, where a thrilling instrument makes an OK toy. Tiny violins are shrill. Their shrieks are musical mice. The color of a mechanical clock is lost in translation. Whatever you're telling me sounds like the straight teeth of rodents. My dreams throw the book at the varmint. We both shudder as the dictionary thuds. You've got to admit, our Esperanto's hopeless. Your virgin is unfaithful. My savory hero boards the ship of Marco Polo, loaded with soy from Ohio.

Variation on a Theme Park

My Mickey Mouse ears are nothing like sonar. Colorado is far less rusty than Walt's lyric riddles. If sorrow is wintergreen, well then Walt's breakdancers are dunderheads. If hoecakes are Wonder Bras, blond Wonder Bras grow on Walt's hornytoad. I have seen roadkill damaged, riddled and wintergreen, but no such roadkill see I in Walt's checkbook. And in some purchases there is more deliberation than in the bargains that my Mickey Mouse redeems. I love to herd Walt's sheep, yet well I know that muskrats have a far more platonic sonogram. I grant I never saw a googolplex groan. My Mickey Mouse, when Walt waddles, trips on garbanzos. And yet, by halogen-light, I think my loneliness as reckless as any souvenir bought with free coupons.

We Are Not Responsible

We are not responsible for your lost or stolen relatives. We cannot guarantee your safety if you disobey our instructions. We do not endorse the causes or claims of people begging for handouts. We reserve the right to refuse service to anyone. Your ticket does not guarantee that we will honor your reservations. In order to facilitate our procedures, please limit your carrying on. Before taking off, please extinguish all smoldering resentments. If you cannot understand English, you will be moved out of the way. In the event of a loss, you'd better look out for yourself. Your insurance was cancelled because we can no longer handle your frightful claims. Our handlers lost your luggage and we are unable to find the key to your legal case. You were detained for interrogation because you fit the profile. You are not presumed to be innocent if the police have reason to suspect you are carrying a concealed wallet. It's not our fault you were born wearing a gang color. It is not our obligation to inform you of your rights. Step aside, please, while our officer inspects your bad attitude. You have no rights that we are bound to respect. Please remain calm, or we can't be held responsible for what happens to you.

Wino Rhino

For no specific reason I have become one of the city's uni-corns. No rare species, but one in range of danger. No mythical animal, but a common creature of urban legend. No potent stallion woven into poetry and song. Just the tough horny beast you may observe, roaming at large in our habitat. I'm known to adventurers whose drive-by safari is this circumscribed wilderness. Denatured photographers like to shoot me tipping the bottle, capture me snorting dust, mount on the wall my horn of empties that spilled the grape's blood. My flesh crawls with itchy insects. My heart quivers as arrows on street maps target me for urban removal. You can see that my hair's stiffened and my skin's thick, but the bravest camera can't document what my armor hides. How I know you so well. Why I know my own strength. Why, when I charge you with my rags, I won't overturn your sporty jeep.

Wipe That Simile Off Your Aphasia

as horses as for
as purple as we go
as heartbeat as if
as silverware as it were
as onion as I can
as cherries as feared
as combustion as want
as dog collar as expected
as oboes as anyone
as umbrella as catch can
as penmanship as it gets
as narcosis as could be
as hit parade as all that
as icebox as far as I know
as fax machine as one can imagine
as cyclones as hoped
as dictionary as you like
as shadow as promised
as drinking fountain as well
as grassfire as myself
as mirror as is
as never as this

Recyclopedia (2006)

Trimmings (1991)

Don't ask me what to wear

attributed to Sappho

Becoming, for a song. A belt becomes such a small waist.
Snakes around her, wrapping. Add waist to any figure, sub-
tract, divide. Accessories multiply a look. Just the thing, a
handy belt suggests embrace. Sucks her in. She buckles.
Smiles, tighter. Quick to spot a bulge below the belt.

Lips, clasped together. Old leather fastened with a little
snap. Strapped, broke. Quick snatch, in a clutch, chased
the lady with the alligator purse. Green thief, off relief, got
into her pocketbook by hook or crook.

Tender white kid, off-white tan. Snug black leather, second skin. Fits like a love, an utter other uttered. Bag of tricks, slight hand preserved, a dainty. A solid color covers while rubber is protection. Tight is tender, softness cured. Alive and warm, some animal hides. Ghosts wear fingers, delicate wrists.

Starving to muffler moans, boa scarfs her up. Feathers tickle her nose. Kerchief, fichu. Gesundheit.

Her red and white, white and blue banner manner. Her red and white all over black and blue. Hannah's bandanna flagging her down in the kitchen with Dinah, with Jemima. Someone in the kitchen I know.

Brimming over eye shades cool complexion, delicate hue, the lid on, keeps a cool head under high hat

A little tight, something spiked, tries on a scandal. One of a pair vamps it up with a heel. If the shoe fits, another mule kicking, a fallen, arch angel loses sole support.

Two shapely legs stretch, then run. Sheer magic, a box divided. One saw a woman cut in half, waving incredible feet.

A light white disgraceful sugar looks pink, wears an air,
pale compared to shadow standing by. To plump recliner, naked
truth lies. Behind her shadow wears her color, arms full of
flowers. A rosy charm is pink. And she is ink. The mistress
wears no petticoat or leaves. The other in shadow, a large,
pink dress.

The color 'nude,' a flesh tone. Whose flesh unfolds barely, appealing tan. Shelf life of stacked goods. Body stalking software inventories summer stock. Thin-skinned Godiva with a wig on horseback, body cast in a sit calm.

Garters garnish daughters partner what mothers they gather they tether.

In folds of chaste petticoats, chupamirtos. In a red sack with a silk ribbon, hummingbird, whose tongue is sweet. Charm for love, a captive beat, a flutter. Hidden under ruffles, secret heart, a red pouch tied with silk.

A rich match fits a couple of gilded calves. Silk stockings glide up fine-tuned, high-toned thighs. Blue-vein stock requires noblessing, sitting pretty in lap de luxe.

Bare skin almost, underworn. Warm stitched-together soft torn toy. Stuffed and laced voluptuous imaginary mammal made of lovely lumps. Dear plump-cheeked plaything taken to bed and hugged in the dark.

Releases from valises. Scientific briefs. Chemists model molecular shadows structure mimic dancers. Shirt on the line, a flapper's shimmy shake in a silk chemise. A shift, a woman's movement, a loose garment of manmade fabric. Polly and Esther living modern with better chemistry.

Of a girl, in white, between the lines, in the spaces where nothing is written. Her starched petticoats, giving him the slip. Loose lips, a telltale spot, where she was kissed, and told. Who would believe her, lying still between the sheets. The pillow cases, the dirty laundry laundered. Pillow talk-show on a leather couch, slips in and out of dreams. Without permission, slips out the door. A name adores a Freudian slip.

Night moon star sun down gown. Night moan stir sin dawn gown.

Dress shields, armed guard at breastwork, a hard mail covering. Brazen privates, testing their mettle. Bolder soldiers make advances, breasting hills. Whose armor is brassier.

Mistress in undress, filmy peignoir. Feme sole in camisole. Bit part, petite cliché. Dégagé ladies lingering, careless of appurtenances. Longing pajamas, custom worn to disrobe. Froufrou negligee, rustling silk, or cattle. Negligent in ladies' lingerie, a dressy dressing down.

Girt, a good old girl got hipped. They thrive with wives, broad beams. Most worthy girth, providing firm. Foundations in midriff. Across (between) girdled loins, tender girders. Gartered, perhaps, struts. Stretching, a snap crotch.

Some panties are plenty. Some are scanty. Some or any. Some is ante.

Tiny binary aftermath figure. Navel baste playmates with ultimate breeder of nuclear families. Suburban bombshell shelters magazines of big guns aiming to sell inny things or nothing at all.

Step into gathered floral. Sashay and flounce out. At length, skirt's sweep, her furbelow. Or slit, tight. Gored, wrapped, young shirttail tucked. Cowgirl, hips suede. Leather fringe skirts, a border. A stiff, fine crinoline. Straight seams, hemmed or binding. Warm hands, felt skirt. An issue of blood, she pleated.

Mum, dissembling girl, resembling cartoon mouse. Scantness forces a stand, she cannot bend.

Heartsleeve's dart bleeds whiter white, softened with wear. Among blowzy buxom bosomed, give us this—blowing, blissful, open. O most immaculate bleached blahs, bless any starched, loosening blossom.

Menswear, the britches. Rosie flies off the handle. Jeans so tight, she pants. Wants to cool out, slacks off.

Of what material softness folds to hold her, under when over, inside or out, where air is, makes a difference in motion, living here—or walking. Taking off, putting on her flimsy garment. Holes breathe, and swallow. Openings, hem, sleeve. Borders on edges where skin stops, or begins. Fancy trim. Sew buttons on, but they are slow to open flowers—imagine the color. Loose skirt, a petal, a pocket for your hand. My dress falls over my head. A shadow overtakes me.

When a dress is red, is there a happy ending. Is there murmur and satisfaction. Silence or a warning. It talks the talk but who can walk the walk. Distress is red. It sells, shouts, an urge turned inside out. Sight for sore eyes, the better to see you. Out for a stroll, writing wolf-tickets.

Girl, pinked, beribboned. Alternate virgin at first blush. Starched petticoat besmirched. Stiff with blood. A little worse for wear.

The bride wore white. Posed in modest bodice a la mode. Cake with sugar rosebuds and white frosting. Everyone gets a piece. Off-color jokes, borrowed and blue. Her blush, tip of the iceberg, froze in layers of lace, in a photograph of her smile.

Cold feet, darned socks. Mismatched pair, the black sock and the blue sock. Male color blindness. A girl's thin ankles.

What's holding her up. Straps, laces. Garters, corsets, belts with laces. What's holding them up. If not straps, then laces. Buttons and bows, ribbons and laces set off their faces. Girls in white sat in with blues-saddened slashers. Laced up, frilled to the bone. Semi-automatic ruffle on a semi-formal gown.

Her feathers, her pages. She ripples in breezes. Rim and fringe are hers. Who fancies frills. Whose finery is a summer frock, light in the wind, riffling her pages, lifting her skirt, peeking at edges. The wind blows her words away. Who can hear her voice, so soft, every ruffle made smooth. Gathering her fluttered pages, her feathers, her wings.

Clip, screw, or pierce. Take your pick. Friend or doctor,
needle or gun. A dab of alcohol pats that little hurt hole.
Hardly a dimple is soon forgotten brief sting. Stud, precious
metal. Pure, possessive ring. Antibody testifying with im-
munity to gold, rare thing. So malleable and lovable, wear-
ing such wounds, such ornaments.

Body on fire, spangles. Light to sequin stars burn out at both ends.

Cinderella highball cocktail frock. Plastered, shellacked, and laminated. Blind drunk hobbled home in a lame dress.

Bones knit. Skins pink, flush tight. White margin, ample fleshings. Out of character, full blush. Flushed out of hiding, pink in the flesh.

Gold chains, choker, ring her neck. Draw a bead, string it.
Precious jewel, locket. Real pearl handles it, lacy-necked
in the black. What rankles, she fakes it. Less than naked,
strung out, stranded.

Akimbo bimbos, all a jangle. Tricked out trinkets, aloud galore. Gimcracks, a stack. Bang and a whimper. Two to tangle. It's a jungle.

Harmless amulets arm little limbs with poise and charm.

In feathers, in bananas, in her own skin, intelligent body attached to a gaze. Stripped down model, posing for a savage art, brought color to a primitive stage.

Chichi busy bodice with fancy work got filigreed and gold.
Then plumed themselves in fancy dress and knit their brows
to clothe the naked.

Punched in like slopwork. Mild frump and downward drab. Slipshod drudge with chance of dingy morning slog. Tattered shoulders, frayed eyes, a dowdy gray. Frowzy in a slatternly direction.

Duds, garbled garb. Misfits, women in breaches. Early
bloomers or bluestockings, whose blue worsted wicked
black dress, or a white none inhabits. Unholy Magdalene
with her veil of tears.

Mohair, less nape to crown fluffed pillow. Fuzzyhead, down for a nap. Soft stuff of dreams in which she fluffs it.

Animal pelts, little minks, skins, tail. Fur flies. Pet smitten
smooth beaver strokes. Muff, soft, 'like rabbits.' Fine fox
stole, furtive hiding. Down the road a pretty fur piece.

Opens up a little leg, some slender, high exposure. Splits a
chic sheath, tight slit. Buy another peek experience, price
is slashed. Where tart knife, scoring, minced a sluttish strut.
Laughing splits the seams. Teeth in a gash, letting off steam.

Swan neck, white shoulders, lumps of fat. A woman's face above it all. Unriddled sphinx 'without secrets.' Alabaster bust, paled into significance. Clothes opening, revealing dress, as French comes into English. Suggestively a cleavage in language.

Decorative scrap. A rib, on loan. Fine fabric, finished
at edges. Fit for tying or trimming. Narrow band, satin, a
velvet strip. A ribbon wound around her waist. A glancing
bow. Red ribbon woven through her, blue-ribbon blonde.
For valor, a shred of dignity. A dress torn to ribbons.

For frills, fancy crimps and shaves. Cuts curls, frail frounce.
Smiles, curtsies, now only of women flexing a fondness.
Plain as a broad steaming a wrinkle, takes out the starch.
Frilled up to here, she starts sleeking. Flat, flatter, flatterer.

Gaudy gawks at baubles fondle tawdry laces up in garish gear, a form of being content.

Chaste, apprehended, collared and cuffed. Kept under wraps, as bridal veils visually haze precious, easily torn, gauzy romantic tissues. Thin threads lace into delicate, expensive fabrics woven and unwoven at night by patient spinsters with needles and scissors. Laced in, as fate would have it. Knots and the tiniest holes. Surgical cutting and sewing. Peeking as usual. Skin under lace. A thread, a net effect, a web to sleep in. A white nightgown, girl, child, baby, laced and unlaced. A ruffle, a frill. A pale piece of something, almost made of air.

Rapt babes in peekaboo webs. Preying widows, spiders in black weeds. Smoldering glance in a drop-dead dress. Witches burning at high stakes. Blackened virgins, selling the sizzle.

Hand in glove hankers, waves a white flag. Hand to mouth surrenders, flirts with hanky-panky.

Low impact, lateral moves. No new wrinkles favor grace to last past shoe chat. Old sneakers jog their memories. Cool heels, odd hours in the park. Whistling dogs and cars exhaust. Stopped in her tracks, that doffed hat knocks her socks off.

Shades, cool dark lasses. Ghost of a smile.

A fish caught, pretty fish wiggles for a while. A caught fish squirms. A freshly licked fish sighs. Gapes with holes for eyes. A wiggling fish flashes its display. A pattern over whiteness. Bareness comes with coverage for peeking through holes to see flesh out of water. Cold holes where eyes go. The sea is cold. Her body of foam, some frothy Venus. Or strayed mermaid, tail split, bleeds into the sea. With brand new feet walks unsteady on land, each step an ache.

What a little moonlight inside her pink silvery is softness
condensing a glaze to repair a blister. Itches sit and silken,
growing dearer to the wearer. Who would wear a neck-
lace of tears. Inside her moonlight lining, tears were shed.
Smooth tears, bitter water, a salted wound produced a pearl.
A mother's luster manufactured a colored other. Pearl had
a mother who cried.

Her ribbon, her slender is ribbon when to occupy her
hands a purse is soft. Wondering where to hang the keys,
the moon is manicured. Her paper parasol and open fan
become her multiplication of a rib which is connected
and might start a fire for cooking. Who desires crisp vege-
tables, she opens for the climate. A tomato isn't hard. It
splits in heat, easy. It's seasonal. Once in a while there is
heat, and several flowers are perennials. Roses shining with
green-gold leaves and bright threads. Some threads do wilt
after starching. She has done the starching and the bleach-
ing. She has pink too and owns earrings. Would never be
shamed by pearls. A subtle blush communicates much.
White peeks out, an eyelet in a storm.

Thinking thought to be a body wearing language as cloth-
ing or language a body of thought which is a soul or body
the clothing of a soul, she is veiled in silence. A veiled, un-
available body makes and available space.

S*PeRM**K*T (1992)

This is no authority for the abuse of cheese.

Gertrude Stein

Lines assemble gutter and margin. Outside and in, they straighten a place. Organize a stand. Shelve space. Square footage. Align your list or listlessness. Pushing oddly evening aisle catches the tale of an eye. Displays the cherished share. Individually wrapped singles, frozen divorced compartments, six-pack widows all express themselves while women wait in family ways, all bulging baskets, squirming young. More on line incites the eyes. Bold names label familiar type faces. Her hand scanning throwaway lines.

With eternal welcome mats omniscient doors swing open
offering temptation, redemption, thrilling confessions. The
state of Grace is Monaco. A shrine in Memphis, colossal
savings. A single serving after-work lives. In sanctuaries of
the sublime subliminal mobius soundtrack backs spatial
mnemonics, radiant stations of the crass. When you see it,
you remember what you came for.

Pyramids are eroding monuments. Embalmed soup stocks the recyclable soul adrift in its newspaper boat of double coupons. Seconds decline in descent from number one, top of the heap. So this is generic life, feeding from a dented cant. Devoid of colored labels, the discounted irregulars.

Just add water. That homespun incantation activates potent powders, alchemical concentrates, jars and boxes of abracadabra. Bottled water works trickling down a rainy day watering can reconstitute the shrinking dollar. A greenback garnered from a tree. At two bucks, one tender legal portrait of Saint No-Nicks stands in for clean-shaven, defunct cherry chopper. Check out this week's seasonal electric reindeer luz de vela Virgin Mary markdowns. Choose from ten brands clearly miracle H-2-0. Pure genius in a bottle. Not municipal precipitate you pay to tap, but dear rain fresh capped at spring. Cleaner than North Pole snow, or Commander in Chief's hardboiled white collars. Purer than pale saint's flow of holy beard or drops distilled from sterile virgin tears.

Aren't you glad you use petroleum? Don't wait to be told you explode. You're not fully here until you're over there. Never let them see you eat. You might be taken for a zoo. Raise your hand if you're sure you're not.

Desperately pregnant nubile preferred stock girls deliver perfect healthy psychic space alien test tube babes, in ten or less, or yours is free, we guarantee.

It must be white, a picture of health, the spongy napkin made to blot blood. Dainty paper soaks up leaks that steaks splayed on trays are oozing. Lights replace the blush red flesh is losing. Cutlets leak. Tenderloins bleed pink light. Plastic wrap bandages marbled slabs in sanitary packaging made to be stained. A three-hanky picture of feminine hygiene.

Iron maidens make docile martyrs. Their bodies on the
racks stretched taut. Honing hunger to perfect, aglow in
nimbus flash. A few lean slicks, to cover a multitude, fix a
feast for the eyes. They starve all the things we crave.

Chill out a cold, cold world. Open frost-free fridget. Thaw and serve slightly deferred gratification, plucked from the frozone, hard packed as slab of ice aged mammoth. Cool cache stashed between carbon dated ziplocked leftovers and soothing multicolored safety tested plastic teething ring.

Kills bugs dead. Redundancy is syntactical overkill. A pin-
prick of peace at the end of the tunnel of a nightmare
night in a roach motel. Their noise infects the dream. In
black kitchens they foul the food, walk on our bodies as we
sleep over oceans of pirate flags. Skull and crossbones, they
crunch like candy. When we die they will eat us, unless we
kill them first. Invest in better mousetraps. Take no pris-
oners on board ship, to rock the boat, to violate our beds
with pestilence. We dream the dream of extirpation. Wipe
out a species, with God at our side. Annihilate the insects.
Sterilize the filthy vermin.

A daughter turned against the grain refuses your gleanings, denies your milk, soggy absorbency she abhors. Chokes on your words when asked about love. Never would swallow the husks you're allowed. Not a spoonful gets down what you see of her now. Crisp image from disciplined form. Torn hostage ripening out of hand. Boxtop trophy of war, brings to the table a regimen from hell. At breakfast shuts out all nurturant murmurs. Holds against you the eating for two. Why brag of pain a body can't remember? You pretend once again she's not lost forever.

Nine out of ten docks trash paper or plastic. My shrink
wraps securely stashed and shredded freshness re-enforced
double baggage. All tidy toxic clean dregs folded down
in dumps with safety improved twist-off tops. Crumpled
sheets, sweating ammunition. A strychnine migraine is a
p.r. problem. Every orifice leaks. No cap is tamper proof.

Chow down on all floors. Nuzzle shallow dishes. Swallow spittle lapping muzzles. Doggie style fashions better leather collars. Caressed pets milk bone bandits. Checkerboard square, clean as hound's tooth. Rub a rawhide bone up out back. See Rover choose a rubber toy over puppy kibble. Poodle grooming lather bothers a tick. A bomb goes off to rid a house of pests. Yet pets are loyal and true watch dogs take a licking while nestling birds feather bed and beak fast kisses. Cat nips flannel mouse. Kitty litters kittens.

Plushy soft tissues off screen generic rolls as the world turns on re-vivid revival rewinds reruns recycling itself. A box of blue movie equals smurf sex. Poor peewee couldn't shake it. Wished he had a bigger one. Per inch of clear resolution's color window, more thick squares snag a softer touch.

Two thousand flushes drain her white porcelana, chlorinsed with antistepton disinfunktant unknownabrasives, cleanliness gets next to.

In specks finds nothing amiss. Rubs a glove on lemony wood. But the gleam of a sigh at a spotless rinsed dish. Spots herself in its service, buffed and rebuffed. Shines on the gloss of bird's eye drop leaf maple tabletop. Pledges a new leaf shining her future polishing skills. The silver dropped at dinner announces the arrival of a woman at a fork. She beams at a waxing moon.

What's brewing when a guy pops the top off a bottle or can talk with another man after a real good sweat. It opens, pours a cold stream of the great outdoors. Hunting a wild six-pack reminds him of football and women and other blood spoors. Frequent channels keep high volume foamy liquids overflowing, not to be contained. Champs, heroes, hard workers all back-lit with ornate gold of cowboy sunset lift dashing white heads, those burly mugs.

Off the pig, ya dig? He squeals, grease the sucker. Hack that fatback, pour the pork. Pig out, rib the fellas. Ham it up, hype the tripe. Save your bacon, bring home some. Sweet dreams pigmeat. Pork belly futures, larded accounts, hog heaven. Little piggish to market. Tub of guts hog wilding. A pig of yourself, high on swine, cries all the way home. Streak o' lean gets away cleaner than Safeway chitlings. That's all, folks.

Well bread ain't refined of coarse dark textures never enriched a doughty peasant. The rich finely powdered with soft white flours. Then poor got pasty pale and pure blands ingrained inbred. Roll out dough we need so what bread fortifies their minimum daily sandwich. Here's a dry wry toast for a rough age when darker richer upper crust, flourishing, out priced the staff with moral fiber. Brown and serve, a slice of life whose side's your butter on.

A dream of eggplant or zucchini may produce fresh desires.
Some fruits are vegetables. The way we bruise and wilt, all
perishable.

Bad germs get zapped by secret agents in formulaic new improved scientific solutions. Ivory says pure nuff and snowflakes be white enough to do the dirty work. Step and fetch laundry tumbles out shuffling into sorted colored stacks. That black grape of underwear fame denies paternity of claymate raisinets. Swinging burgers do a soft shoe, gringo derbies tipping Latina banana. Some giggling lump of dough, an infantile chef, smiles animatedly at his fresh little sis. They never gets a tan in the heartwarming easy bake oven because they is eternal raw ingredients for programmed microwavering half-baked expressions of family love.

Toe jam must 'cause jelly don't. Mink chocolate melts
in you.

Champagne dreams wet shammy softy. Hands-on carwash, a pampering. Bathtub's a cheap vacation. Cruising her archipelago, laid back with turn-on pages. Emerged from placid stacked suds, hyperbolic exotic aisle of glamour bubbles. Pearl diver's paradise. All sparkling steel and spritzed crystal rubbed down clean to the squeak. A body with an interior rolls out sleek waxed shiny hard enameled. It takes her away, that seductive new smell, in fourteen flavors. She's cherry, just driving off the lot.

Eat junk, don't shoot. Fast food leaves hunger off the hook.
Employees must wash hands. Bleach your needles, cook
the works. Stick it to the frying pan, hyped again. Another,
teflon prez. Caught in the fire 'round midnight, quick and
dirty biz. Smoked in the self-cleaning oven.

How anorexics treat themselves. Sucking slim mint for the breathless, rationed yet tingling indulgence. Over-counters prescribe themselves slighter than any other lifetime of fractioned unburned energy hands down all ads up. How fresh in your mouth to eat a sweet thought minus the need to work off guilt, to amortize the cost.

Slow ketchup, slower. Dark coffee, darker. Nice white rice.
Meat is real. Clean meat. Trimmed, not bloody.

Past perfect food sticks in the craw. Curdles the pulse. Coops up otherwise free ranging birds whose plucked wings beat hearts over easy. Flapping aerobically, cocks walk on brittle zeros. They make and break and scramble to get ahead. Whisk the yokels into shape. Use their pecker order to separate the whites.

Seeds in packets brighter than soup cans, cheaper than lottery tickets, more hopeful than waxed rutabagas, promising order in alphabetized envelopes, dream startled gardens one spring day tore open. Sown in good dirt, fingered tenderly.

Ad infinitum, perpetual infants goo. Pastel puree of pure
pink bland blue-eyed babes all born a cute blond with no
chronic colic. Sterile eugenically cloned rows of clean rosy
dimples and pamper proof towhead cowlicks. Adorable
babyface jars. Sturdy innocent in the pink, out of the blue
packs disposing durable superabsorbent miracle fibers. As
solids break down, go to waste, a land fills up dead diapers
with funky half-life.

Refreshing spearmint gums up the words. Instant permkit combs through the wreckage. Bigger better spermkit grins down family of four. Scratch and sniff your lucky number. You may already be a wiener.

Hide the face. Chase dirt with an ugly stick. That sinking sensation, a sponge dive. Brush off scum on some well scrubbed mission. It's slick to admit, motherwit and grit ain't groceries.

Flies in buttermilk. What a fellowship. That's why white
milk makes yellow butter. Homo means the same. A woman
is different. Cream always rises over split milk. Muscle men
drink it all in. Awesome teeth and wholesale bones. Our
cows are well adjusted. The lost family album keeps saying
cheese. Speed readers skim the white space of this galaxy.

Muse & Drudge (1995)

Fatten your animal for sacrifice, poet,
but keep your muse slender.

Callimachus

Sapphire's lyre styles
plucked eyebrows
bow lips and legs
whose lives are lonely too

my last nerve's lucid music
sure chewed up the juicy fruit
you must don't like my peaches
there's some left on the tree

you've had my thrills
a reefer a tub of gin
don't mess with me I'm evil
I'm in your sin

clipped bird eclipsed moon
soon no memory of you
no drive or desire survives
you flutter invisible still

another funky Sunday
stone-souled picnic
your heart beats me
as I lie naked on the grass

a name determined by other names
prescribed mediation
unblushingly on display
to one man or all

traveling Jane
no time to settle down
bee in her bonnet
her ants underpants

bittersweet and inescapable
hip signals like later
some handsome man kind on the eyes
a kind man looks good to me

I dream a world
and then what
my soul is resting
but my feet are tired

half the night gone
I'm holding my own
some half forgotten tune
casual funk from a darker back room

handful of gimme
myself when I am real
how would you know
if you've never tasted

a ramble in brambles
the blacker more sweeter juicier
pores sweat into blackberry tangles
going back native natural country wild briers

country clothes hung on her all and sundry
bolt of blue have mercy ink perfume
that snapping turtle pussy
won't let go until thunder comes

call me pessimistic
but I fall for sour pickles
sweets for the heat
awrr reet peteet patootie

shadows crossed her face
distanced by the medium
riffing though it
too poor to pay attention

sepia bronze mahogany
say froggy jump salty
jelly in a vise
buttered up broke ice

sun goes on shining
while the debbil beats his wife
blues played left-handed
topsy-turvy inside out

under the weather
down by the sea
a broke johnny walker
mister meaner

bigger than a big man
cirrus as a heart attracts
more power than a loco motive
think your shit don't stink

edge against a wall
wearing your colors
soulfully worn out
stylishly distressed

battered like her face
embrazened with ravage
the oxidizing of these
agonizingly worked surfaces

that other scene offstage
where by and for her he descends
a path through tangled sounds
he wants to make a song

blue gum pine barrens
loose booty muddy bosom
my all day contemplation
my midnight dream

something must need fixing
raise your window high
the carpenter's here
with hammer and nail

what you do to me
got to tell it
sing it shout out
all about it

ketchup with reality
built for meat wheels
the diva road kills
comfort shaking on the bones

trouble in mind
naps in the back
if you can't stand
sit in your soul kitsch

pot said kettle's mama
must've burnt them turnip greens
kettle deadpanned not missing a beat
least mine ain't no skillet blonde

sue for slender
soften her often
mamiwata weaves
rolexical glitter

get a new mouth
don't care what it costs
smell that hot sauce
shake it down south

the purify brothers
clamor for rhythm
ain't none of they business
'til the ring is on the finger

breaks wet thigh high stepper
bodacious butt shakes
rebellious riddem
older than black pepper

déjà voodoo queens
rain flooded graves in New Orleans
sex model dysfunction
ruint a guest's vacation

figures with lit wicks
time to make a switch
rumba with chains removed
folkways of the turf

black dispatch do do run run
through graffiti brierpatch
scratch a goofered grapevine telegraph
drums the wires they hum

mad dog kiwi antifreezes
green spittle anguished folks
downwind skidrowed elbow greasers
monkey wrench nuts and bolts

my skin but not my kin
my race but not my taste
my state and not my fate
my country not my kunk

how a border orders disorder
how the children looked
whose mothers worked
in the maquiladora

where to sleep in stormy weather
Patel hotel with swell hot plate
women's shelter under a sweater
friends don't even recognize my face

tombstone disposition
is to graveyard mind
as buzzard luck
to beer pocketbook

the backwoods deflated whip
blank North American skies
rag dolls made of black scraps
with pearl button eyes

random diva nation of bedlam
headman hoodlum doodling
then I wouldn't be long gone
I'd be Dogon

down there shuffling coal
humble materials hold
vestiges of toil
the original cutting tool

splendid and well-made
presenting no disturbance
the natural order of things
between man and himself

try others but none lasted
a shame they went that way
missing referents murking it up
with clear actors lacking

too tough is tough enough
to walk these dirty streets with us
too loud too strong too black bad
too many desires you've never met

butch knife
cuts cut
opening open
flower flowers flowering

scratched out hieroglyphs
the songs of allusion
and even the motion
changing of our own violins

cough drops prick thick
orange ink remover inside
people eating tuna fish
treat the architecture to pesticides

elaborate trash
disparaged rags
if I had my rage
I'd tear the blueprint up

chained thus together
voice held me hostage
divided our separate ways
with a knife against my throat

black dreams you came
sleep chilled stuttering spirit
drunk on apple ripple
still in my dark unmarked grave

ain't cut drylongso
her songs so many-hued
hum some blues in technicolor
pick a violet guitar

emblems of motion
muted amused mulish
there's more to love
where that came from

heavy model chevy of yore
old time religion
low down get real down
get right with Godzilla

write on the vagina
of virgin lamb paper
mother times mirror
divided by daughter

soulless divaism
incog iconicism
a dead straight head
the spectrum wasted

dicty kickpleat
beats deadbeats
hussified dozens
womanish like you groan

belly to belly
iron pot and cauldron
close to home
the core was melting

head maid in made out
house of swank kickback
plaçage conquer bind
lemon melon mélange

if you've been in Virginia
where the green grass grows
did you send your insignia
up a greased flagpole

you used to hock your hambone
at a cock and bull pawnshop
got your start as a sideman
now you're big on your own

what makes tough muffins
pat Juba on the back
Miz Mary takes a mack truck in
trade for her slick black cadillac

la muerte dropped her token
in the subway slot machine
nobody told the green man
the fortune cookie lied

keep your powder dry
your knees together
your dress down
your drawers shut

a picture perfect
twisted her limbs
lovely as a tree
for art's sake

muse of the world picks
out stark melodies
her raspy fabric
tickling the ebonies

you can sing their songs
with words your way
put it over to the people
know what you doing

curly waves away blues navy
saved from salvation
army grits and gravy
tries no lie relaxation

some little bitter
spilled glitter
wiped the floor
with spoiled sugar

back dating double dutch
fresh out of bubble gum
half-step in the grave
on banana peels of love

devils dance on a dime
cut a rug in ragtime
jitterbug squat diddly bow
stark strangled banjo

how you feel when it's windy
something blue on you
speak to the feeling
consolate your mind

many strong and soon
these seeds open wings
float down parachutes
then try one more again

copulation from scratch
kisses go down hard
no weekday self
makes it bleed

edges sharpened
remove the blur
enhance the image
of dynamic features

dark-eyed flower
knuckling under
lift a finger for her
give the lady a hand

not her hard life
cramped hot stages
only her approach
ahead of the beat

live in easy virtue
where days behaving send
her dance and her body
forward to a new air dress

a pad for writing
where dreams hit el cielo
crack the plaster fool mood rising
it's snowing on the radio

honey jars of hair
skin and nail conjuration
a racy make-up artist collects herself
in time for a major retrospection

her lady's severe beauty
and downright manner
enhance the harsh landscape
positioned with urban product

mule for hire or worse
beast of burden down when I lay
clean and repair the universe
lawdy lawdy hallelujah when I lay

tragic yellow mattress
belatedly beladied blues
shines staggerly avid diva
ruses of the lunatic muse

odds meeting on a bus
the wrecked cognition
calling baby sister
what sounds like abuse

you have the girl you paid for
now lie on her
rocky garden
I build her church

a world for itself
where music comes to itself
three thirds of heaven
sure to be raining

on her own jive
player and instrument
all the way live
the way a woman might use it

sugar shack full
of fat sweaty ladies
women of size with men
who love too much

what is inward
wanting to get out
prey to the lard
trying to pass for butter

cakewalk matrix
tapping the frets
dubbed and mastered
tucked into the folds

kiss my black bottom
good and plenty
where the doorknob split
the sun don't shine

it's rank it cranks you up
crash you're fracked you suck
shucks you're wack you be
all you cracked up to be

dead on arrival
overdosed on whatever
excess of hate and love
I sleep alone

if you were there
then please come in
tell me what's good
think up something

psychic sidekick
gimme a pigfoot
show me my lifeline
read me my rights

in Dahomey the royal umbrella
roof sky tree dome
heads up the procession of saints
balling the jack back home

framed in her snake-relief decorated doorway
bordered with zigzag deer legs
the notched beam is a stepladder
dried millet a sign of hospitality

this art is fast disappearing
indigenous pigments learned from their mothers
earth from the river
fingers and hands

men harnessed mules
rode hard put away wet
on the brine sea
unwed men toss and sweat

dark rain laden clouds
fragrant womb
from pyramid to palm
the black tide of mud

calabash of water
botanica Yoruba
latecomers to a potboiler
plot rebellion in the quarter

under the drinking gourd
they stood in a word
free despite thirst
lovely in their dust

torn veins stitched
together with pine needles
mended hands fix
the memory of a people

go ahead and sing the blues
then ask for forgiveness
you can't do everything
and still be saved

update old records
tune around the verses
fast time and swing out
head set in a groove

felt some good sounds
but didn't have the time
sing it in my voice
put words in like I want them

noise in the market
my mustang done slowed down
tore up bad now
put a ruination on it

bring money bring love
lucky floorwash seven
powers of Africa la mano
poderosa ayudame numeros sueños

restore lost nature
with hoodoo paraphernalia
get cured in Cuban by a charming
shaman in an urban turban

forgotten formula cures
endemic mnemonic plague
statisticians were sure
the figures were vague

sister mystery listens
helps souls in misery
get to the square root
of evil and render it moot

wine's wicked wine's divine
pickled drunk down to the rind
depression ham ain't got no bone
watermelons rampant emblazoned

island named Dawta
Gullah backwater
she swim she fish
here it be fresh

cassava yuca taro dasheen
spicy yam okra vinegary greens
guava salt cod catfish ackee
fatmeat's greasy that's too easy

not to be outdone she put
the big pot in the little pot
when you get food this good
you know the cook stuck her foot in it

they pass their good air
mixed with fresh fair
complex ions somewhere
frimpted frone she's stand alone

female of the specifically
human woman not called
by dog or dug by some tool—no fool who
takes stray pets or rakes implements for complements

what I do with my hats
they make their own parade
of float and glitter like birds
adorn the open umbrella

my dreams could take
advantage of me and no
one would tell me because
they don't know where to reach me

mothers have spawned
what warriors now own
cruel emblems and secrets
divulged only to the adept

signs in the heavens
graphemes leave the trees
turning over fresh pages
of notation: a choreography for bees

cooter got her back scratched
with spirit scribble
sent down under water
with some letters for the ancestors

the folks shuffle off
this mortal coffle and
bamboula back to
the motherland

why these blues come from us
threadbare material soils
the original colored
pregnant with heavenly spirit

stop running from the gift
slow down to catch up with it
knots mend the string quilt
of kente stripped when kin split

white covers of black material
dense fabric that obeys its own logic
shadows pieced together tears and all
unfurling sheets of bluish music

burning cloth in a public place
a crime against the state
raised the cost of free expression
smoke rose to offer a blessing

with all that rope they gave us
we pulled a mule out of the mud
dragging backwoods along
in our strong blackward progress

she just laughs
at weak-kneed scarecrow
as rainbow crow flies
over those ornery cornrows

everlasting arms
too short for boxers
leaning meaning
signifying say what

Ethiopian breakdown
underbelly tussle
lose the facts just keep the hustle
leave your fine-tooth comb at home

if your complexion is a mess
our elixir spells skin success
you'll have appeal bewitch be adored
hechizando con crema dermoblanqueadora

what we sell is enlightenment
nothing less than beauty itself
since when can be seen in the dark
what shines hidden in dirt

double dutch darky
take kisses back to Africa
they dipped you in a vat
at the wacky chocolate factory

color we've got in spades
melanin gives perpetual shade
though rhythm's no answer to cancer
pancakes pale and butter can get rancid

the essence lady
wears her irregular uniform
a pinstripe kente
syncopation suit

she dreads her hair sprung from lock down
under steel teeth press gang
galleys upstart crow's nest

eyes lashed half open
look of lust bitten
lips licked the dusky
wicked tongued huzzy

am I your type
that latest lurid blurb
was all she wrote
her highbrow pencil broke

self-made woman gets
the hang—it's a stretch
she's overextended weaving
many spindly strands on her hair loom

walking through the alley
all night alone
stalked by a shadow
throw the black cat a bone

step off bottom woman
when the joint gets jinky
come blazing the moment
the hens get hincty

raw souls get ready
people rock steady
the brown gals in this town
know how to roll the woodpile down

dry bones in the valley
turn over with wonder
was it to die for our piece
of buy 'n' buy pie chart

hot water cornbread
fresh water trout
God's plenty the preacher shouts
while the congregation's eating out

women of honey harmonies offer
alfalfa wild flower buckwheat and clover
to feed Oshun who has sweet teeth
and is pleased to accept their gift

these mounts that heaven touched
saints sleep in their beds
distress is hushed by dream when
they allow the bird to lift their heads

ain't your fancy
handsome gal
feets too big
my hair don't twirl

from hunger call
on the telephone
asking my oven for
some warm jellyroll

if I can't have love
I'll take sunshine
if I'm too plain for champagne
I'll go float on red wine

what you can do
is what women do
I know you know
what I mean, don't you

arrives early for the date
to tell him she's late
he watches her bio clock balk on seepy time
petals out of rhythm docked for trick crimes

flunked the pregnancy test
mistimed space probe, she aborted
legally blind justice, she miscarried
scorched and salted earth, she's barren

when Aunt Haggie's chirren throws
an all originals ball
the souls ain't got a stray word
for the woman who's wayward

dead to the world
let earth receive her piece
let every dark room repair her heart
let nature and heaven give her release

moon, whoever knew you
had a high IQ until tonight
so high and mighty bright
poets salute you with haiku

fixing her lips to sing
hip strutters ditty bop
hand-me-down dance of ample
style stance and substance

black-eyed pearl around
the world girl
somebody's anybody's
yo-yo Fulani

occult iconic crow
solo mysterioso
flying way out
on the other side of far

the royal yellow sovereign
a fragile grass stained widow
black veins hammered gold
folded hands applaud above a budding

flat back green and easy
stacked for salt meat seasoning
some fat on that rack
might make her more tasty

a frayed one way slave's
sassy fast sashay
fastens her smashing essay
sad to say yes unless

your only tongue turns
me loose excuse my French
native speaker's opening act
a tight clench in the dark theater

software design for
legible bachelors
up to their eyeballs
in hype-writer fonts

didn't call
you ugly—said
you was ruined
that's all

pass the paperbag
whether vein tests
the wild blue
blood to the bone

spin the mix fast forward
mutant taint of blood
mongrel cyborg
mute and dubbed

poor stick doll
crucifix stiff
bent bird shutters
torn parasol

mellow elbow lengthy
fading cream and peaches
bleach burn lovingly
because she's worth it

ass is grassy ass is
ashy just like we do
such subtle cuts
clutter the difficult

trick rider circuity
wash your mariney
lick and promisory
end of story morning-glory

dressed as a priestess
she who carries water
mirrors mojo breasts
Yemoja's daughter

some loose orisha gathering
where blue meets blue
walk out to that horizon
tie her sash around you

how many heads of cowries
openmouthed oracles
drinking her bathwater
quench a craving for knowledge

kumbla of red feathers
tongues chant song
may she carry it well
and put it all down

tom-tom can't catch
a green cabin
ginger hebben
as ancestor dances in Ashanti

history written with whitening
darkened reels and jigs
perform a mix of wiggle
slouch fright and essence of enigma

a tanned Miss Ann startles
as the slaver screen's
queen of denial a bottle
brown as toast Egyptian

today's dread would awe
Topsy undead her missionary
exposition in what Liberia
could she find freedom to study her story

up from slobbery
hip hyperbole
the soles of black feet
beat down back streets

a Yankee porkchop
for your knife and fork
your fill of freedom
in Philmeyork

never trouble rupture
urban space fluctuates
gentrify the infrastructure
feel up vacant spades

no moors steady whores
studs warn no mares
blurred rubble slew of vowels
stutter war no more

get off your rusty dusty
give the booty a rest
you must be more than just musty
unless you're abundantly blessed

I can't dance don't chance it
if anyone asks I wasn't present
see I wear old wrinkles
so please don't press me

my head ain't fried
just fresh rough dried
ain't got to cook
nor iron it neither

you've seen the museum of famous hats
where hot comb was an artifact
now it's known that we use mum or numb our stresses
sometimes forget to fret about our tresses

heard about that gal
in Kansas City got meatballs
yes you shall have cake and eat
your poundcake on the wall

quickie brick houses
don't roll rickrack stones
or bats eyelashes rocks
you 'til bric-a-brac's got no home

ain't had chick to chirp nor child to talk
not pot to piss in, no dram to drink
get my hands on money marbles and chalk
I'll squeeze 'til eagle grin, 'til pyramid wink

tussy-mussy mufti
hefty duty rufty-tufty
flub dub terra incog
mulched hearts agog

hooked on phonemes imbued with exuberance
our spokeswoman listened for lines
heard tokens of quotidian
corralled in ludic routines

slumming umbra alums
lost some of their parts
getting a start
in the department of far art

monkey's significant uncle
blond as a bat
took off beat path
through tensile jungle

dark work and hard
though any mule can
knock down the barn
what we do best requires finesse

frizzly head
gumbo clay
skull drudgery
mojo handyman

crow quill and India
put th' ink in think
black cat in the family tree
hairy man's Greek to me

krazy kongograms
recite the fatal bet
missiles of affection
dingbat flings brick velvet

bean pole
lightning rod
bottle tree
tall drink

go on sister sing your song
lady redbone senora rubia
took all day long
shampooing her nubia

she gets to the getting place
without or with him
must I holler when
you're giving me rhythm

members don't get weary
add some practice to your theory
she wants to know is it a men thing
or a him thing

wishing him luck
she gave him lemons to suck
told him please dear
improve your embouchure

tomboy girl with cowboy boots
takes coy bow in prom gown
your orange California suits
you riding into sundown

lifeguard at apartheid park
rough, dirty, a little bit hard
broken possum poke a possum
park your quark in a hard aardvark

a wave goodbye a girl
bred on the Queen Mary
big legged gal
how come you so contrary

let the birds pick her
make a nest of her hair
let the root man conjure
her to stare and stir air

sauce squandering sassy cook
took a gander bumped a pinch of goose
skinned squadroon cotillion filled
uptown ballroom with squalid quadrille

don't eat no crow, don't you know
ain't studying about taking low
if I do not care for chitterlings
'tain't nobody's pidgin

Hawkins was talking
while I kept on walking
now I'm standing in my tracks
stepping back on my abstract

if not a don't at least a before
skin of rubber chicken
these days I ignore
I'm less interested in

gaudy colors you flaunt
how loud you sirens behave
the man drowns in your salt
you revive him with a wave

restless born-agains
outlaw beat machines
yet the drums roll on
let the churchy femmes say amen

downhome quotes
the human figure
carries the vote
over dead signatures

tasty brown sugar molasses
accused of wide abandoned laughter
nothing left to lose or gain
delicate powder melts in the brain

ass can't catch
mere language
sings scat logic
talking shit up blues creek

no miss thing
ain't exactly rude
just exercising
her right to bare attitude

rope rash lads
rubber whiplashed
breakneck beauty
can be had

money's mammy mentions
some chit chat
getting paid
to take it like that

singed native skin
binging island sun
shines on shingles
shunning unhinged singles

ghetto-bound pretos
call on dark petro
powers that be fighting
when there's no money to lighten

historic old haunts where
creole servants get the door
or sweep up dusty graveyards
with zombi esprit décor

tropical fantasy
punany as you want to be
coked bottled bodies
with fantacide faces

mutter patter simper blubber
murmur prattle smatter blather
mumble chatter whisper bubble
mumbo-jumbo palaver gibber blunder

colored hearing colored
sounds darker
back vowels lower
down there deeper

churn and dasher
mortar and pestle
bumped your head
on a piece of cornbread

I didn't went to go
swing slow zydeco
so those green chariots
light your eyes up

massa had a yeller
macaroon a fetter
in his claptrap
of couth that shrub rat

sole driver rode
work hard on demand
he's the man
just as long as he can

outside MOMA
on the sidewalk
Brancusi's blonde
sells ersatz Benin bronzes

Joe Moore never
worked for me—oh moaner
you shall be free
by degrees and pedigrees

handheld interview cuts to
steady voice over view
extra vagrants gobble up the scenery
this camera's gonna roll all over you

discarded barnacled bard
grinning with bad dentures
remembering coonskin adventures
in your hackneyed backyard

solar flares scrambled
bell bottoms sunnyside
signal didn't she ramble
those black holes backslide

drippy tresses bagged
in plastic do-rag
sensible heel in execu-drag
whose dress sucks excess

O rose so drowsy in
my flower bed your pink
pajamas zig-zag into
fluent dreams of living ink

carve out your niche
reconfigure the hybrid
back in kitchen
live alone, buy bread

your backbone slip
sliding silk hipped
to the discography
of archival sarcophagi

pregnant pause conceived
by doorknob insinuation
and onset animal
laminates no DNA

manx cat rations
pussy got your tongue
angoraphobic X-man
sex kitten operation

blow hair died
a natural death
laid aside glory fried
flashing a panacea

her realness
was wild at the time
leastwise they tell me
it was legendary

chez lounge lizard
hip-hop hazard
master beats and breaks
baby's back-up aches

a strict sect's
hystereotypist hypercorrects
the next vexed hex
erects its noppy text

where whirly Saturn
turns worldly girls
wear curly perms
affirm natty pattern

chenille feely zeroes
fuzzy nooky fumble
your nu-nile omieros
our frondy jungle

lucky lucre dream dujour
a lotto numbing ventured dues
paid off a doler
and another don't

rap attacks your tick
cold fusion's licks
could make you sick
nobody's dying in this music

womanish girl meets mannish boy
whose best buddy's a doggish puppy
he dictate so dicty, she sedate so seditty
the girl get biggity when the boy go uppity

I'm down to Saint James Infirmary
getting tested for HIV
the needle broke, the doctor choked
and told me I'd croak from TB

did I say nobody's dying
well I lied, like last night
I was lying with your mama who was crying
for all the babies born in Alabama

marry at a hotel, annul 'em
nary hep male rose sullen
let alley roam, yell melon
dull normal fellow hammers omelette

divine sunrises
Osiris's irises
his splendid mistress
is his sis Isis

creole cocoa loca
crayon gumbo boca
crayfish crayola
jumbo mocha-cola

warp maid fresh
fetish coquettish
a voyeur leers
at X-rated reels

spaginzy spigades
splibby splabibs
choice voice noise
gets dress and breath

slave-made artifact
your salt-glazed poetry
mammy manufacture
jig-rig nitty-gritty

fast dance synched up so
coal burning tongues
united surviving ruin
last chance apocalypso

broke body stammering spirit
been worked so hard
if I heard a dream
I couldn't tell it

pipsqueak at sea
snail shell matrices
whirlwind gig
minkisi indigo

rose is off the bloomers
storm in the womb
an old broom scatters
shotgun rumor

hip chicks ad glib
flip the script
spinning distichs
tighter than Dick's hatband

buttermilk haystack
woodpile inkwell
darktown brierpatch
buckwheat bottom sugarhill

mulatos en el mole
me gusta mi posole
hijita del pueblo moreno
ya baila la Conquista

chant frantic demands
in the language
bring generic offerings
to a virgin of origins

yes I've tried in vain
never no more to call your name
and in spite of all reminders
misremembered who I am

ghosts brush past
surprise arrival at
these states of flux
that flow and flabbergast

cross color ochre with stalk of okra
that prickly lover told her
she tastes like an Okie
yet lacks the rich aroma of a smoker

those cloudy days I'd fly
from the icy airport
while you tried to breathe life
into your bucktoothed scarecrow

if you turned down the media
so I could write a book
then you could look me up
in your voluminous recyclopedia

raped notes torn
as deep ones parted
the frank odor of the rodeo
the reason a person

pretend you don't understand
reckless letters I wrote
can't read my crooked hand
decode those cryptic notes

you were longing to belong
thoughts wander where have you gone
Zuli made her bed at home
that's why we don't get along

her red flag is flying
with bright sequins shining
her heart of swords
is its own reward

feed the spirits or they'll
chew on your soul
you'll be swallowed and digested
by a riled-up crocodile

married the bear's daughter
and ain't got a quarter
now you're playing the dozens
with your uncle's cousins

sitting here marooned
in limbo quilombo
ace coon ballooned up
without a parachute

use your noodle for
more than a hat rack
act like you got the sense
God gave a gopher

couldn't fold the tablecloth
can't count my biscuits
think you're able to solve
a figure, go ahead and risk it

when memory is unforgiving
mute eloquence
of taciturn ghosts
wreaks havoc on the living

intimidates intimates
polishing naked cactus
down below a bitter buffer
inferno never froze over

to deaden the shock
of enthusiastic knowledge
a soft body when struck
pale light or moderate

smooth as if by rubbing
thick downward curving
bare skin imitative
military coat made of this

mister arty martyr
a jackass to water
changing partners
in the middle of a scream

bereft of flavor
for lack of endeavor
he chooses a heifer
and loses forever

delirious boozer
he smoothes her sutures
removes a moocher
from her future

a thing of shreds and patches
hideous scarecrow she
puts teeth in any nightmare
of the man who sleeps with matches

slashing both your wrists
to look tough and glamorous
dead shot up in the art gallery
you can keep your shirt on already

while I slip into something more funkable
rub-a-dub with rusty man abrasions
was I hungry sleepy horny or sad
on that particular occasion

invisible incubus took up
with a cunning succubus
a couple of mucky-mucks
trying to make a buck

slandered and absurdly slurred
wife divorced her has-been
last man on earth hauls ass to the ash can
his penis flightier than his word

precious cargo up crooked alleys
mules and drugs
blood on the lilies
of the fields

drive by lightning
let Mississippi rip
catch some sense
if you get my drift

watch out for the wrecking crew
they'll knock you into the dirt
your attic will be in your basement
and you'll know how it feels to be hurt

a planet struck by fragments
of a shattered comet
tell it after the break
save it for the next segment

tabloid depravity
dirty snowball
held together
with weak gravity

"fool weed, tumble your
head off—that dern wind
can move you, but
it can't budge me"

he couldn't help himself
he couldn't help it
he couldn't stop himself
nobody stopped him

blessed are stunned cattle
spavined horses bent under their saddles
blessed is the goat as its throat is cut
and the trout when it's gutted

Jesus is my airplane
I shall feel no turbulence
though I fly in a squall
through the spleen of Satan

in a dream the book beckoned
opened for me to the page
where I read the words
that were to me a sign

houses of Heidelberg
outhouse cracked house
destroyed funhouse lost
and found house of dead dolls

two-headed dreamer
of second-sighted vision
through the veil
she heard her call

they say she alone smeared herself
wrote obscenities on her breast
snatched nappy patches from her scalp
threw her own self on a heap of refuse

knowing all I have is dearly bought
I'll take what I can get
pick from the ashes
brave the alarms

another video looping
the orange juice execution
her brains spilled milk
on the killing floor

if she entered freely
drank freely—did that not mean
she also freely gave herself to one and all—
then when was she no longer free?

we believed her
old story she told
the men nodded at her face
dismissing her case

debit to your race
no better for you—lost
gone off demented
throwing unevenhanded

disappeared undocumented workhorse
homeless underclass breeder
dissident pink collard criminal
terminal deviant indigent slut

riveted nailed to the table
crumpled muddied dream stapled
in her face mapped folded back
to the other side of the facts

that her body bleeds
is no surprise
a fragment bursts and color seeps
through her camouflage

bannered behind her
braid unfurled
extended she lean aiming
breaking the ribbon

kink konk crisp crinkle
my monkey's off his head
he wears my hat that
helps me think a little

zipped into high-tech overalls
suited to her lightfoot boots
kicking her heels up
and away beyonder

just as I am I come
knee bent and body bowed
this here's sorrow's home
my body's southern song

cram all you can
into jelly jam
preserve a feeling
keep it sweet

so beautiful it was
presumptuous to alter
the shape of my pleasure
in doing or making

proceed with abandon
finding yourself where you are
and who you're playing for
what stray companion

Broken Glish (2013)

Antarctica

Your coolness thaws this lowly clod, the superficial earth's
unbuckled equator. You steep the bliss of arctic mammals in
congealing arteries of barren ice. You throw the brakes on ancient
glaciers to hone the polar bear's survival skills. You've become a
colorless target unable to mend a mortal wound.

Broken Glish

Finding myself in the desert, I planted a luminous seed. I let go a howl past moist teeth, certain it couldn't have been the mute sunshine laughing, a sane cello, or a brand-new brain. No one came near. Nor was I ever shallow or newsworthy to you, as the moon has revealed. Only a murmur blasted by brief springs, by the dry impenetrable glare of a taproot. I fell asleep on rational sand dunes, where the cactus rasped above my toenails, a solid stench descending from oblivion. Slowly, unlike the spines I was stuck with, I spoke calmly, addressing the watery ocean I'd discovered in my dotage—and I went on undeterred, healed by that unwavering stink.

Devil's Ashtray

Who empties the devil's ashtray? Who in hell is laundering his dirty shirts? Whose job is it to lick the devil's pots and polish his spittoons? Would you believe it? Some are paid to do his work while others volunteer.

Immaterial

Your nebula loiters with none of a father's abandonment, blotting out stars. Dark holes in heaven stand still. Oh, to be brilliantly agitated while swallowing somber dusk. Yes, you—your famished bones plunged into doldrums. Your slight skin never anesthetized. We wait serenely as large black triangles betray immeasurable time. Forever adrift, you are mutable as blandness turning vivid. Surely, in the infinity of a single grain, you keep your balance. Leaning away from specks of matter you never were, you merge with a gas giant. A stable, unique blob stitched together from whole cloth, an unspoken image from the sunken depth of unknown dimensions.

Not Dead Yet

You hate missing nothing. Not ignorant eyes of potato, clean air, clear lungs, or white gloves poised for inspection. Yet you skip bits of plankton that swim in infinite acres of ice cubes. So, you miss the genie escaping like Houdini, or the only locust in a field of hybrid corn. You favor dry basements, sharp pencils, and a tame patch of earth that looks rather flat.

Urban Tumbleweed:
Notes from a Tanka Diary
(2013)

On Starting a Tanka Diary

My tanka diary began with a desire to strengthen a sensible habit by linking it to a pleasurable activity. I wanted to incorporate into my life a daily practice of walking and writing poetry. As committed as I am to writing, I needed a break in my routine, so I determined to alter my sedentary, unconsciously cramped posture as a writer habitually working indoors despite living here in "sunny California." With a pen and notebook tucked into my pocket, I could escape from the writer's self-imposed confinement, if only to walk from home to the local post office. With the tanka diary to focus my attention, a pedestrian stroll might result in a poem. Merging my wish to write poetry every day with a willingness to step outdoors, my hope was that each exercise would support the other.

Now I look forward to this daily reminder that head and body are connected. Most days I go for short walks in various parts of Los Angeles, Venice, and Santa Monica, or longer hikes in the canyons on weekends with friends. I also lead student poets on "tanka walks" in the Mildred E. Mathias Botanical Garden on the campus of UCLA. At other times I explore unfamiliar neighborhoods as I travel. Trips to the botanical garden are opportunities for learning the names of plants from all over the world that have found a home here in California, a place defined as much by non-natives as by its native species.

Like many inhabitants of Los Angeles, I am not native to this state of elemental seasons: wind, fire, flood, mudslide and earthquake. Like ice plant, eucalyptus, and nearly all of L.A.'s iconic palm trees, I too am a transplant to this metropolis of motor vehicles with drivers who regard, and are regarded by, pedestrians and cyclists as road hazards. Walking instead of driving allows a different kind of attention to surroundings. Each outing, however brief, becomes an occasion for reflection. Los Angeles, however urban, offers everyday encounters with nature.

So I began the diary despite being able to recognize only the most common creatures, and feeling that I lack a proper lexicon to write about the natural world, when what we call natural or native is more than ever open to question. I did not turn into an amateur naturalist or avid birdwatcher, but I became a bit more aware of my environs. The 366 tanka verses collected represent a year and a day of walking and writing.

This is a record of meditations and migrations across the diverse terrain of southern California's urban, suburban, and rural communities, its mountains, deserts, ocean and beaches. In greater Los Angeles my walks can range from downtown streets and alleys to spectacular natural landscapes to outdoor shopping malls. Also noted are differences of climate and geography as I travel to other states. Parts of the tanka diary were written during a month-long residency in Marfa, Texas, sponsored by the Lannan Foundation. Others were written during a visit to Sweden where I was invited to participate in Världspoesidagen, Stockholm's celebration of World Poetry Day.

This work is my adaptation of a traditional form of Japanese syllabic verse. A tanka is a brief poem of 31 syllables, originally printed as a single line of text. The line is subject to internal division of semantic and syllabic units. When written in English it is customary to break the tanka into five lines, approximating its fixed pattern of syllables (5-7-5-7-7). My limited knowledge of the form is based on reading translations of a few classical and modern Japanese poets, along with contemporary tanka composed in English.

While embracing the notational spirit of this tradition, I depart from established convention in both languages, choosing instead a flexible three-line form with a variable number of syllables per line. I try to adhere to the 31-syllable limit, although I am aware that the number of syllables in a given word can vary, depending on the speaker and the circumstances. "California," for example, sometimes has four syllables, at other times, five.

The brevity and clarity of tanka make it suitable for capturing in concise form the ephemera of everyday life. With refined awareness of seasonal changes and a classical repertoire of fleeting impressions, Japanese traditional poetry contemplates, among other things, the human being's place in the natural world, an idea I wanted to explore in my own nontraditional way.

What is natural about being human? What to make of a city dweller taking a "nature walk" in a public park while listening to a podcast with ear bud headphones? What of a poet who does not know the proper names of native and non-native fauna and flora, who sees "a yellow flower by the creek"—not a *Mimulus*?

Keep straight down this block,
then turn right where you will find
a peach tree blooming

Richard Wright

Look about you. Take hold of the things that
are here. Let them talk to you.

George Washington Carver

The morning news landed in the driveway, folded,
rolled, and rubber-banded, wrapped in plastic
for protection from the morning dews.

By midday the ardent sun burns through
the chilly morning fog and cloudy haze that weather
reporters call "May gray" and "June gloom."

Wear hat and sunglasses. Dress in layers. Peel off
clothing from morning to high noon. Put shirt
and jacket back on after sundown.

Instead of scanning newspaper headlines,
I spend the morning reading names
of flowers and trees in the botanical garden.

Each sweeping branch of California buckeye
extends a wide green hand,
presenting to the air a feathery white bouquet.

Flowers of evergreen tree called bottlebrush,
not stiff bristles but velvety filaments,
leave fingers brushed with yellow pollen.

Did early settlers risk brewing a deadly
cup of mud when they roasted and boiled
bitter seeds of the Kentucky coffee tree?

Blackfoot daisy's dark foliage withstands extreme
heat and drought, with bright-eyed flowers
that bloom almost year-round.

Flame tree, I must have missed your season
of fire. All I see are your ashy knees, your kindling
limbs, branches of extinguished blossoms.

Purple jacaranda blooms, spectacular
on branches overhead. Underfoot,
a sticky mess where they land on the sidewalk.

Awakened too early on Saturday morning
by the song of a mockingbird
imitating my clock radio alarm.

Folded cardboard tent-shaped trap
hanging among dark leaves of the lemon tree
to capture the galling Mediterranean fly.

Chain link fence, locked gate protect this urban
garden. Fugitive fragrance of honeysuckle
escapes to tempt the passing stranger.

Bird of paradise, a potted plant in
florist shop windows. Here in my yard
it grows with no help from me, and a head taller.

Why should I care about my neighbor's
riotous dandelions? Does he concern himself
with my slovenly jacaranda?

Walking along the green path with buds
in my ears, too engrossed in the morning news
to listen to the stillness of the garden.

Shy extrovert entices and repels
with petals and thorns. Modest exhibitionist
hides her blush under a pink ruffle.

Even in this landscaped paradise
people buy fresh-cut flowers, considered
more aesthetic than the ones growing in the yard.

As parents and children enjoy the park,
a toddler offering bread crumbs to pigeons
turns and runs as the fierce-eyed birds approach.

Shady eucalyptus grove where sleeping
butterflies cover each limb of every tree—
a rest stop on their migratory flight.

We'd planned to hike to the top of the trail
for a breathtaking view of Pacific,
but turned back down at the sight of a rattler.

Paparazzi snap snoozing celebrities
in stretch limos cruising down Hollywood
Boulevard past anorexic palm trees.

Between train station and high-rises,
he diverts pedestrians, drumming on
plastic buckets and battered metal canisters.

"No hay de queso?" a customer asks *la señora*
selling foil-wrapped homemade tamales
to workers waiting for the bus.

Gazing up at the city's hanging gardens:
concrete walls of freeway overpasses
with overgrown fringes of tangled vines.

Music pounds so boldly through their speakers
we all hear the beat. They're having a blast
and blasting it to everyone in earshot.

A bruised banana peel, tossed, sprawled out
on the sidewalk—what's so funny about that?
If someone slipped and fell, who would be laughing?

Pedestrians on neighborhood sidewalks,
swerving slightly to avoid smearing a child's
exuberant drawings in colored chalk.

For "curb appeal," neighbors hired a crew
of turf installers; in only two days of labor
they laid down an impressive green lawn.

If you must keep a dog in the city, you've got to go
out for walks. If you must stop
at my house, please pick up your pooch's poop.

.

With daily commuters, an extra passenger
on the bus. Ladybug clinging to the window
didn't need to pay a fare.

From a distance, wrecked cars on the freeway
are crumpled toys, the helicopter
circling up above, a curious dragonfly.

Parking in front of the apartment block,
the produce truck driver whose horn announces
his arrival with "La Cucaracha."

Looking up at the sky to estimate
my mood, as if to calculate the sum
of all clouds subtracted from the total blue.

Bare feet at ocean's edge of dark, wet sand,
run toward, then away from frothy waves
as small birds feed on invisible insects.

On the beach house deck we sat at sunset
to watch the blazing Frisbee fall into the ocean
without a splash or a sizzle.

Networks of tree roots, sinewy tentacles
cracking sidewalks, pushing up bulges
in asphalt streets, clogging city sewer lines.

Along the roadside, someone has spilled
pink Styrofoam peanuts. They add color
to the grassy green, but I still prefer flowers.

A noisy crowd gathers every afternoon.
Crows on the roof, in the trees, on the lawn,
all with exciting news to crow about.

Remember summers loafing in a hammock
between two trees while a citronella coil
burns itself into an ashen snake?

Orange and yellow marigold flowers
manufacture a natural insect repellant.
In sweltering heat, you smell it.

Families avoid the beaches after heavy rains.
Swimmers stay away from the waves.
Our city gutters drain to the ocean.

For the middle of July in a drought-stricken
year, more than a few lawns in the neighborhood
are looking incredibly green.

Squirrel, stretching yourself out flat
to cool your belly on a shaded rock. On hot days
do you wish your fur coat had a zipper?

That painful summer heat of August when you burn
your hand grasping the metal doorknob
at the entrance of a house facing west.

Ferny leaf with fragrant pink silky fluff shades
their café patio table. Their words
mix together like citrus and champagne.

Blast of hellish breath, infernal scourge,
parched wind that whips and scorches. Green
torches, oily eucalyptus trees, bursting into flame.

Pilots drop tons of water and fire
retardant on two-hundred-foot flames
engulfing juniper, oak, and ponderosa pine.

Diminutive green-gold fans, wavering
with the faintest breeze, each languid leaf
of the gingko tree lets me feel a bit cooler.

Instead of seeing stars in the sky at night,
look for bold city lights and celestial bodies
posed on Hollywood sidewalks.

No tree in sight to shade us from the searing
glare, that cloudless day in Chinatown,
you stopped to buy a paper parasol.

Clean dirt marks the path, lined with white
stones, winding through the well-tended park,
leading to a rippling stream created for our pleasure.

The determination of a turtle
clambering out of a pond, up the slippery
side of a rock to rest in the sun.

Found on my walk today, rumpled greenbacks
dropped under a tree will reimburse me
for crisp dollars that I lost another day.

Bamboo, jointed like my finger, pointed at the sky.
What fine fishing poles you'd make for the girl
who spent hours dreaming at the lake.

Like a firefly, a charming erratic friend,
delightful to see, yet you wouldn't
depend on it for reading the newspaper.

Two seagulls face off in the parking lot
between Costco and In-N-Out,
quarreling over a half-eaten hamburger bun.

Hiking up Topanga Canyon trail,
we spoke of bobcats, coyotes, and rattlesnakes—
but only harmless lizards crossed our path.

Yes, it is legal to harvest the overhanging fruit
of your neighbor's avocado tree.
Just don't smuggle it out of state.

If I could hold this bowl of blue to cracked
lips, if to quench this desert thirst I could
swallow the sky, would I choke on carbon clouds?

Don't need picket fences, brick wall,
or razor wire. Our home's protected by
prickly pear cactus and thorny bougainvillea.

Native or not, you're welcome in our gardens.
Lavender's dress is not so vibrant as your
green trousers and purple velour sleeves.

Although they grow best in sunny places
with moist but well-drained earth, daylilies
are tolerant of many conditions and soils.

In high school biology class my
laboratory partner took apart the frog
while I observed and took accurate notes.

Water trickles down on clean white flower,
star of five petals sheltered under green leaves
held up like cupped hands to catch the raindrops.

My visitor from Nebraska buys
a sack of assorted seashells at a souvenir shop,
then scatters them along the beach.

They steal from city streets, sell to metal recyclers
anything from bronze statues to street lamps,
fire hydrants, and manhole covers.

All water is recycled—though "toilet to tap"
was an unfortunate slogan for
the municipal water treatment plant.

I have shamelessly neglected all of the succulent
jades and aloes you planted around the patio—
and they have thrived.

Honeybees delve in, their tailpipes
tipping up into view as their heads disappear
into the fluff of cheerfully red pompoms.

Before it was known as recycling, they were
making huarache sandals with thick black
rubber soles fashioned from re-used tire treads.

A profusion of oleanders—to beautify
the freeway and filter the air, though
leaf, stem, and blossom all are poison.

Los Angeles isn't always this smoggy, you know.
There are days the sky is so clear
you can see the HOLLYWOOD sign from here.

My reckless shadow, landing on the twelve-lane
freeway down below this pedestrian bridge,
playing chicken with oncoming cars.

On the commuter train, using her camera
phone instead of a mirror, she draws
on her lips a "sinfully scarlet" smile.

Her Silver-Tongued Companion

Four brisk legs scissor-walking into the garden:
a quick black cat cutting through straight green
stems and folded leaves of blank white tulips.

Hummingbird alters its course, zooming
closer to check out the giant hibiscus flower—
only me in my red summer dress.

Dark-centered petals, purple coneflower,
tall parasol for fuzzy soft lamb's ear
and green-silvery stalks of dusty miller.

Here we have neighborhoods where apricot,
fig, and citrus trees are grown for show, where ripe
to bursting fruit is left to drop and rot.

When you complain about the worm
in your salad bowl, our server assures us,
"That is how you know the lettuce is organic."

Those many years ago I imagined green hair
of fir tree, handshake of friendly palm,
melancholy tears of weeping willow.

293

In my room at El Bonito, nicknamed
"Elbow," what a previous guest left behind
resembles a different body part.

"No, thanks," she said when he offered
a sip from his flask. "You'd look good in
a bikini," he told her as she waited for the bus.

I'm not homeless. I'm a bum. I was living
in luxury, making plenty money.
But I gave it all up for alcohol.

Encyclopedia set with a few missing
volumes, snaggleteeth in enormous
jaws of a prehistoric fossil shark.

Sirens in the distance, voices of
two men arguing, the unmistakable sound
of someone vomiting in the alley.

Office memos send notice of ants invading
the sugar bowl kept in the coffee break room,
lost bees swarming in the stairwell.

A Venice Beach sculptor caresses
wet sand to make a shapely mermaid.
He charges each tourist a fee to take her picture.

Seafood restaurants called Something's Fishy
and Killer Shrimp. An actor wearing
a frog costume waves a sign for Ugly Sushi.

Would have said this purple clustered flower
looks like a burst of fireworks, but of course it's
the fireworks that imitate the flower.

Throughout the year we exist in dazzling drought.
When the rare cloudburst occurs, we complain
about getting caught and drenched in the rain.

Adorned with snakes around his neck
like jewelry, he knows that the most beautiful
reptiles are not always the most venomous.

On Santa Monica's beach they're worshipping
a different saint. Wading in white, the chanters
launch small boats with gifts for Yemanjá.

Urban tumbleweed, some people call it,
discarded plastic bag we see in every city
blown down the street with vagrant wind.

Long ago, meat fell off the bones, animal
simmered in broth or stew of primordial
ooze, skeleton of woolly mammoth.

Non-native ice plant on postage stamps
represents the golden state like a governor
whose tongue gets tangled in California.

Paramedics check vital signs as
emergency room doctors prepare for
the arrival of amateur mycologists.

Often they are immigrants, who've gathered,
cooked, and eaten toxic death caps resembling
tasty wild mushrooms of their native land.

Within a small family of survivors
the cost of a grandparent's funeral
is divided between two credit cards.

Lovers of nature, when you're wandering
in the pathless wilderness and you meet
a grizzly bear, don't insist on shaking hands.

We sit still in the parked car, enchanted
to see among landscaped flowers a brown
hummingbird spangled with iridescent green.

Feeding on a single weed, its habitat
dwindling, can the caterpillar afford to be
so choosy with its appetite?

Several species of elegant butterflies
are known to be attracted to mountains
of dung and decomposing garbage.

As if they might be learning a new dance,
elders plant their feet on steady ground,
gathering wind in their arms to move cloud hands.

They shook lower branches of the tree
to loosen the tight fruit, back in those days when
they could not wait for hard green plums to ripen.

On a perfect afternoon for puppet theater
in the park, the children laugh, cheer,
and sing along with monkey and zebra.

Plastic flamingo with spinning whirly-gig
wings, backstroking in a stiff wind;
standing up but going nowhere fast, in reverse.

With the click of a mouse you sent me
a picture you got from someone who thought
you'd like a picture of a cat clicking a mouse.

A cop guards the bridge I cross to catch
my bus. He watches as I slow my walk
to stare at the president's car passing below.

Self-guided missile striking its target in the eye:
bee landing in the buttery yellow
center of creamy white petals.

Go ahead and pat me down with human
hands. Don't put me through that machine
with remote controls for electronic strip searches.

Until they crossed the country to that place
of rigid cold, they didn't know cascades
and tumbling waterfalls could freeze in mid-flow.

Turning suddenly, the man walking ahead
caught me staring at his pants that looked
as if he must have put them on backwards.

It merely looks bedraggled, that gangling garden
of rogue roses with stems untrimmed.
It doesn't stir the heart like a true wild rose.

I can't help feeling at war with the elements,
under this fierce onslaught of rain,
with just a sad umbrella as sword and shield.

Not falling into infinite night of stars, but marks
of a black pencil, sketching dimensions,
depths, and shades of moody darkness.

With essential ingredients of air, fuel,
and spark, someone who can build a blazing
fire will always have a source of warmth.

A flurry begins with a solitary snowflake
drifting down reluctantly,
as if afraid to fall alone to earth.

Pine tops, holly berries, boxwood growing
outdoors. An everlasting aluminum tree
with puffs of spun snow displayed indoors.

Figures inside a snow globe, unperturbed
by the blizzard, feet planted firmly, no matter
how they're shaken and turned upside down.

A crack of thunder wakes me in the night,
and now, with a blanket pulled over my head,
I listen to raindrops striking the roof.

Wet and swollen after weeks of steady rainfall,
slick with slime and mold, so on wooden stairs
the visitor slipped and broke her foot.

How does a cold, far-away moon
regulate the implacable tides? Why does
a deep blue devil stand between me and the sea?

Her Silver-Tongued Companion

Returning home tonight, I avoid crushing
a snail that casts a scant shadow
on the wide sidewalk in clear light of a full moon.

Dried lima beans I had left soaking
to cook the next day, forgotten until
a few days later when they had started to sprout.

Storm clouds, ozone, grumble of thunder.
Lightning strike, power surge, electrical outage.
Pitch black, candle flame.

Wracked landscape of writhing worms,
a field of white grass in billowing wind. Think
of the whale's skeleton wrapped in a polar bear coat.

Even the chilliest winter day
at Santa Monica beach is still warm enough
for surfers in wet suits to hug the waves.

The fury of the storm uprooted a venerable
pine tree on the neighbors' lot
and shoved it into the roof of their house.

These colorful little stucco houses in
Sunkist Park don't look so bright today
beneath this overcast sky of cloudy gray.

A shivering dog left out in the rain,
dripping wet and cold as a miserable
werewolf, each raindrop a silver bullet.

Though they can't help flaunting their
vulnerability, I imagine that creeping snails
are trusting me to spare their fragile shells.

We're jerked awake as helicopter blades beat air.
Light glares from above. An amplified shout
orders a fleeing suspect to halt.

My usual half-hour bus ride to work took
two hours today because the president
returned for another fundraiser.

Technological worker bees patrol relentlessly,
chase and sting the enemy, while skilled beekeepers
never leave the nest.

Snippets of fresh green herbs from
a kitchen garden enhance the reputation
of the cook who makes a simple omelet.

At the entrance to the botanical garden,
a sign hung on the gate forewarns: "Slow down.
Watch for turtles on the roads and paths."

So light and delicate, skimming tips
of maidenhair trees. I thought you were butterflies.
Now I see you are the tiniest birds.

In my hotel room in Columbus, Ohio,
an arrangement of flowering weeds
plucked from the Olentangy River trail.

Handcrafted pasta on the menu
has a sauce made with hen of the woods—
mushrooms that herbalists use to resist infection.

Their celebration of spring begins
when the festival's fresh princess is crowned
with a circlet of newly picked asparagus.

If you are perfectly still when it hovers near,
you'll hear it hum; small engine with rapid
wings, a bird no bigger than your thumb.

Waiting for the bus, a girl with plush pink
rabbit ears to match her spring outfit—
not sure what kind of bunny she's supposed to be.

Shabby (never chic) sofa hauled out
to the curb for trash when he noticed its stains
are indelible and it smells like a dog's bed.

Whiff of just-cut young grass, notes of spring
with bracing citrus, distilled and bottled
to create the designer's signature fragrance.

Because of the drizzling rain, you listened
to the sound of the wind. There, for a brief moment,
you found shelter under boughs of pines.

As one beauty encounters another, how lovely
to see the butterfly powder itself
with the flower's dusty pollen.

Grape-sized, egg-shaped, orange-colored citrus:
how strange, at first, eating whole tart-sweet fruit
with thin skin and all, biting into a kumquat.

Never as audacious as the squirrels
that sit up and beg for buttered popcorn,
the chipmunks are so shy we rarely see them.

Clicking through images downloaded
from your camera. Those buskers haven't finished
playing, and already they're in your archive.

Very late in the spring, after every living
bush and shrub had bloomed, you finally found
the strength to display a few green leaves.

Deferential to the stern blustering wind,
slender blades of grass and pliant stalks
of flowers, bowing their heads in its presence.

I wonder who left this scruffy old teddy bear
wedged between bars of a metal fence,
looking as if it's breaking out of jail.

This curly cloud don't grow straight or need
straightening. It takes rough wind to wreck the 'do.
To some, when brushed and combed it still looks tangled.

You could say I am borrowing light
from the moon when I write my tanka
after reading translations of Princess Shikishi.

Enjoying the lingering sweet-tingling
scent, I don't wash my hands right away
after peeling and eating a thick juicy orange.

Jogging along the avenue with sporty
baby strollers, they are lean and sleek in
spandex pants, proving themselves fit parents.

Suddenly orchids in bloom
no longer were rare exotic luxuries,
but sold at tempting prices in the corner market.

I leave traces of ink on paper. Others
can't resist spray-painting a boulder
or carving their names in the skin of a tree.

Contemplate layered petals of a rose until
the rapture begins. Meditate on the lotus
from now until nirvana.

Gang of Buddhist monks in the crosswalk
as yellow turns red—saffron and pomegranate
robes with running shoes and rugged sandals.

Yesterday we talked about your favorite
poem. Today you brought a gift
of fully ripe persimmons in a paper bag.

Tasting artisan chocolates,
hard to choose between Shangri-La
with goji berries or Aztec flavored with smoky chilies.

If heavenly angels want glorious instruments
to announce their arrival, they may pluck them
from the golden trumpet tree.

With all the appealing spaces on
a university campus, I wonder why
they chose this dull spot for their daily prayers.

I follow the bloody red footprints back to
their source—casual mayhem of smashed
ketchup packets smearing the gritty sidewalk.

On Venice Boulevard, men selling oranges,
women selling flowers—vendors wilting
in the sun, sweating out pungent juices.

Looking as if they might be crying,
drivers traveling west at sunset, squinting
because they have forgotten their dark glasses.

We smell rain coming, see dark clouds
and lightning before we hear thunder, watch
storms arrive, wait to get wet before running indoors.

It was no joke, but a question of survival—
the jay-walking rooster, a chicken
crossing the road in rush hour traffic.

Do they lie down still in soft grass
to gaze up at a sky of roaming shape-shifting
clouds? Do children still have time for daydreaming?

Dried-out snake on the road
I brought as a curiosity to the child—
who insisted we give it a proper funeral.

I go for weeks without eating meat,
but sniffing the smoky aroma of barbecued ribs,
I revert back to carnivore.

Alcohol cleans tar from flip-flops. Peanut butter gets
chewing gum out of your hair. Tomato juice
rinses the stink of a skunk.

"Where does California's produce go?"
shoppers ask in supermarkets stocked
with Mexican avocados and Chinese garlic.

Alluring flesh with soft downy skin
that tickles and teases. Sun-warmed cheek
of tawny peach entices you to taste its sweetness.

On the porch, serenaded by a cricket choir—
so charming! Lying in bed, the chirp
of a single cricket—so annoying!

Ninety-nine dashing dots crisscross
the walk, red ants converging on a spot where
someone's dropped a greasy bite of pepperoni.

We keep heating up, so if we're about
to reach our melting point, this could be
the tip of the iceberg that brings us to a boil.

The fence surrounding our family garden
saves lettuce and carrots from hungry
rabbits who like salad as much as we do.

A story from my mother's girlhood:
Dining with friends, she asked for her favorite
piece of chicken, was told, "Rabbits don't have wings."

Mom grew these leafy collards in her organic
garden. She picked them this morning.
Tonight they go well with our cornbread and yams.

She wonders why that misled redheaded
woodpecker keeps flying back to tap-tap-tap
on her house with aluminum siding.

The rental house transformed into enchanted cottage,
its entry way shaded with sinuous vines
of giant honeysuckle.

Upside-down reflection on the pond's
clear surface that I saw before noticing
the deer itself, camouflaged in muffled woods.

Winking fireflies never would compare themselves
to stars and galaxies. Each luminous creation
is stellar in its own realm.

Aloe vera plant in sunny kitchen window,
cool and soothing first-aid treatment
for scorched fingers of an absent-minded cook.

One thing after another: a tired old tree
topples over in the yard, turning on
the water faucet and flooding the lawn.

We awoke to their racket. Tough guys in the alley
fighting over the spoils. Then one raccoon
chased the other out to the street.

We judge the clarity of your eye and press
our fingers against your flesh to guess how long
it's been since you were pulled from the sea.

I managed to do it only that one time when
my grandfather taught me how to bait a fish hook
with a squirming wet earthworm.

Baby ducklings trailing mother duck
can scarcely wet their feet in shallow puddles
of this city's concrete rivers and creeks.

Having lost count of all our risings
and settings, we're now unable to remember
how many times we've saluted the sun.

Summer sparks, lifted up from yellowing
grass, scattered by wind. Flying up to higher
branches of pine trees, cardinals alight.

As each day becomes briefer, each night's darkness
lingers longer, we savor the deep-blushing flesh
and wine-red juice of blood oranges.

Several gallons of chemicals from the hotel pool
get poured through the wrong grate,
sickening a crowd of subway commuters.

A bobcat walked into a bar, wandered
into a saloon, entered a drinking
establishment. Everyone else skedaddled.

Clinics displaying the five-leaf marijuana plant,
weeds sprouting up more numerous than
coffee shops with the mermaid logo.

A corpulent cigar lit up in a blaze of
Old Glory—what patriotic product
is the zeppelin advertising?

Today I give thanks for grace and mercy
bestowed upon me as I go on living,
like a turkey the president pardoned.

Airline passenger detained was no
fanatic hiding explosives, but a smuggler
with expensive lizards in his pants.

Avoid brittle dried goosefoot sold in packets
in grocery stores. Search for fresh epazote
at the outdoor farmers markets.

Jagged leaf, used by Mexican cooks
to flavor beans and combat flatulence;
in large doses epazote is poisonous.

The space station smelled nothing like
an alpine mountain forest or a country meadow,
but those were places he traveled in his dreams.

I'm scanning the path, wary of poison oak
and tangled roots, but also looking
to find a simple treasure: a heart-shaped stone.

Along a familiar hiking trail I recognize
agave, sage, the summer-blooming yucca,
and sticky monkey flower.

The day I notice, returning from my walk,
a hole worn through the heel of one sock,
my thoughtful sister has sent me a new pair.

I'm seeing lots of dead zebras lately
on floors of elegant homes pictured in
interior decorator magazines.

                            Pilots are grounded. Airplanes are afraid
                            to fly. What saboteur hid the fatal trees?
                            What terrorist slept beneath the glacier?

Volcanic ash clouds give a glimpse of
a possible future when no jet planes will fly,
except in emergencies such as war.

Inspired by swarms of oily insects: "If you
can't beat them, eat them," said the inventive
chef who created the locust pizza.

Shared liver of conjoined twins,
chemically preserved in a specimen jar,
in a museum of medical oddities.

Teams of ingenious student engineers
compete annually to design, build, and launch
the most seaworthy concrete canoe.

In the charming ruins of this rock-walled castle,
we could play chess with pebbles while listening
to the sparrows in Shakespeare's garden.

Ambling across the stone bridge over
a still pond covered with green skim,
I knew I would find no quieter place to be alone.

Lavender honey melts in boiling water.
Together they release unfolded flavors
of dried leaves and flowers in my cup.

Shallowest grave for the squirrel, lying still
at the foot of a tree, where I gathered leaves
to cover that small broken body.

At the Round Top, Texas poetry festival
I find that I can live comfortably
in a log house that's air conditioned.

After hearing that poem from my tanka diary,
you handed me a smooth and pleasing stone
shaped like a lopsided heart.

As guests are arriving I see in a corner
of the ceiling the spider's tidy web
that mocks my attempt at housekeeping.

The list of recently discovered
zoological specimens includes a flat-
faced frogfish and a carnivorous sponge.

Our best beach days are steely-gray, cloudy
and cool. We wear our thickest sweaters and listen
to the salty crunch of boots on sand.

Something had to be done, and something
must have been done to rid the campus
of its once booming population of feral cats.

I suppose I'd become a vegetarian
if I had to kill my food. It's been ages
since I've tried to cook a lobster.

What do we call this chimerical creature
possessing hair of a dog, rabbit foot,
shark fin, elephant tusk, and rhino horn?

No, sweet light crude oil and saltwater
don't mix well at all. What's worse, they make
a terrible toxic dressing for oysters and fish.

Bees and yellow jackets are more than
hard workers. They're also soccer fans,
filling the air with the hum of their vuvuzelas.

Envisioning a snow-capped mountain top
where glacier had melted, this determined painter
climbed up to the peak and sprayed it white.

I've lost track of the twisted tale:
the war criminal, the supermodel, and
those "dirty little stones," the uncut diamonds.

A woodchuck is consulted for the weather forecast.
In other news, an octopus predicts
the winner of a soccer match.

Incident at Hollywood and Vine: Los Angeles
City firefighters rescue man caught
under train, struck by Metro Red Line.

"Oh no, not whale meat again," the Japanese
students murmured, complaining about
their lunches in the school cafeteria.

"We proudly harvest rainwater"—a sign
in a neighbor's yard. With a deep barrel
I could humbly and thankfully harvest rain.

Poked with a fingertip, it rolls into a ball.
Crawling across your open hand,
the legs of a doodlebug tickle your palm.

Behind the science building, facing a row
of vending machines, a squirrel holding
in its paws a shiny candy wrapper.

Thigh-high in water, the woman in Sri Lanka,
"This whole road's a river, so no wonder
a crocodile's on my verandah."

As the tidal wave gathered strength,
a fisherman headed his boat out to sea,
to be flung back into life by the tsunami.

Before turning to ice, polar explorer
wrote his wife about their son,
"Get the boy interested in the natural world."

Stockholm guidebooks note, in case you were
wondering, that Svartmangatan wasn't named
for a black man, but for a man dressed in black.

White chimneys wearing stovepipe hats top
rustic red cottages, built for broom makers
and rock blasters, on steep hills of Södermalm.

Wandering lost in Stockholm's twilight streets,
at last I recognize a helpful sign:
TOMATO in the toothpaste over Slussen.

I've packed my text. They've checked the mikes.
My words unfold and now behind my back
my earthy language has become an alien tongue.

What did I bring home from Sweden?
Ham sandwich that the dog sniffed, the inspector
confiscated. Grit collected from Stockholm streets.

Thin air mail envelope with indecipherable
handwriting; I tear it open
to release an inky blue butterfly.

A man disguised as a baggy cow
steals twenty-six gallons of milk from Walmart,
then gives it all to strangers outside the store.

Fourteen exotic birds, lulled asleep, bagged
and taped to the body of the smuggler
arrested in the airport customs line.

Hopeless escape, wild animal keeper
setting the captives loose in Zanesville, Ohio
before shooting himself in the head.

The closest we got to nature: red fruit
floating above city skyline
on label of 2-liter bottle of Cherry Coke.

You may wrap yourself in silk pajamas
after nibbling your coverlet,
chenille caterpillar lounging on a tender leaf.

A "valet" parks your car at the supermarket.
A "beach butler" reserves your plot of sand
with folding chair and bright umbrella.

The police and health departments want
to find out who's been dumping human waste
in the streets of Venice and Santa Monica.

In early morning hours, workers with a pick-up
truck make frequent stops, collecting
shopping carts left on the streets the night before.

Wet droplets falling on faces of church
congregation as the father strides down the aisle
sprinkling holy water and bless-yous.

That homeless woman who hated my shoes
last week—now she lets me buy her
a cup of her favorite mango frozen yogurt.

Stone-ground flour from co-op bulk bins
brings dusty moths that hatch in my kitchen canister
and fly out when I want to bake biscuits.

Behind crumbling walls of ruined adobe,
above radiant orange zinnias,
hummingbirds are aerial acrobats.

Neglected, lapsed in memory, declined,
dilapidated, fallen into decay,
crumbled into dust, returned to nature.

Stranger here and even more out of place
than I am, sapphire blue peacock
promenading down Waco Street in Marfa, Texas.

A spectacular storm on the way to El Paso;
four lanes of traffic halted by
a jack-knifed truck that skidded in the rain.

A kind friend sent me a hastily scribbled note,
inquiring about my "tanka dairy."
I wrote back to say, "I'm milking it."

Along the two-lane desert highway,
solitary Joshua trees appear at regular intervals,
like posted mile markers.

Here we imagine how we might perish: by lightning
strike or snakebite, drowned in a flash or
parched and shriveled in withering heat.

We drive a borrowed car to Pueblo Market
to get our rice and pinto beans,
avocados, jalapeños, and popsicles.

Stately pedestrians, they claim the right of way
on any street, and now wild turkeys on the lawn
chase me back into the house.

Our guided tour ends with outdoor works
of the cantankerous artist; concrete boxes
set in a landscape of "Chinati beige."

A pink snake racing across the desert
hardly needs explanation, unless
you believe it is only a trick of the mind.

On one spiny paddle of the dusty cactus plant
a single yellow flower spreads its petals
for a thirsty hummingbird.

They're meant to underscore boredom or an awkward
silence: recorded cricket chorus
or desert wind rolling a tumbleweed.

It wasn't a bat. Only smudged wings of a giant
moth colliding with your face, startling
as daylight surrendered to shadows.

Had I stayed longer, I might have seen
or maybe smelled a pack of peccaries—
rank javelinas tipping through the neighborhood.

There I went, leaving only my footprints.
Returning, I brought back nothing but
the dust that clings to the sole of a wanderer.

A green streak swooshed across the sky
with a shower of brilliant blue sparks. A boulder
hurled from heaven breaking apart in earth's air.

When I am blazing ghost animated by motion
capture and you the wind inhaling words
then how on earth do you read me?

Florida's cook-off contest to popularize
recipes for lion fish, wild boar,
and python—the state's invasive species.

Why accept what nature gave us?
We're designing our own vegetables so
no regulator can make us eat broccoli.

A year after the triple disaster,
a ghost ship's crossed the Pacific,
but farmers may never return to Fukushima.

Hibernating reptiles and amphibians
awaken in spring when rattlers become
restless and turtles think of traveling.

Mother of octuplets turns down the lead role
in a porn film, but agrees to pose
"tastefully nude" for a tabloid magazine.

The size of a man's hand, covered with
warts. Alarming creatures may have beguiling
eyes, but it's hard to fall in love with a toad.

Standing his ground in a pair of elegant
leather shoes, offering each passer-by
a chance to buy the homeless newspaper.

At night our tidy clean green park is locked
to keep out rough sleepers who bed down on sidewalks
next to shopping carts full of rubbish.

Visiting with us in Los Angeles, our friend
went out for a sunny walk, returned with
wrists bound, misapprehended by cops.

Meandering through hill-top neighborhood
of splendid old mansions, I loiter at wrought-iron gates
picketing the senator's home.

Nothing better to do, I imagine, than try
to get back to sleep after waking
in the slack of night from a tiresome dream.

When you see me walking in the neighborhood,
stopping to admire your garden, I might be
composing a tanka in my head.

Trapped and hunted to the edge of
extinction, gone for nearly ninety years
when a lone gray wolf appears in California.

At first, the dog walker mistook it for a horror
movie prop—that severed head found in the park,
beneath the HOLLYWOOD sign.

Gather loose strands from brush and comb;
roll them into a thick ziggy dreadlock;
mail to an artist who collects the hair of poets.

Eerie mementos of living and dead:
vials of blood in a wooden box,
clumps and curls of hair displayed in plastic bags.

The heart of a saint, stolen from a church
in Dublin. Thieves leave golden chalices,
costly art, choosing this most priceless relic.

They stare as I peer into the window
of a junk shop—bright beady eyes of a
taxidermy wolf with mangy molting fur.

When tainted honeybees become disoriented,
lose their way, and never make it back
to the hive, their colonies collapse.

We'll lasso asteroids as they circle
the planet. We'll find a way to mine
their wealth of aluminum, gold, and platinum.

Woman waiting for a bus to work or walking
early in the morning, beware
the violent man with a teardrop tattoo.

Employees at the county landfill sift
through two weeks of dumpster trash to help
the deputies searching for thrown-away children.

It comes closer, beams brighter, seems fuller
tonight, at this point in its elliptical orbit
around our earth—the super moon.

With darkness as his accomplice,
the blind prisoner finds a way out, slipping
unseen past sentries meant to keep him out of sight.

Arcadius crashed after winning the race.
Cause of death, not drugs but aneurysm.
Vet said, "It could have happened any time."

A bird flew across the border and when
it came to rest, was suspected of being
an alien and possibly a spy.

On a stretch of beach within range
of the military base, two rocks she'd collected
ignited in the pocket of her shorts.

Couldn't prick a pinhole in heavy cover
of cloud to watch the sun, already curtained,
hide itself behind a darkened moon.

A dinosaur can fetch a hefty sum
when the most complete set of well-preserved
tyrannosaurus bones is sold at auction.

Climbers on Everest, so fixed on reaching
their goal they press on beyond fatigue,
passing their predecessors, the frozen dead.

Confronting the suspect, police use lethal
force against a disorderly mountain
lion trespassing in a private yard.

A homeless woman spends her days collecting
odd scraps of paper, then sits in front
of the all-night drugstore, poring over them.

Within territorial boundaries of
contested city blocks, yellow fire hydrants
are marked with graffiti signatures.

In a few billion years Andromeda galaxy
will collide with our Milky Way, but worlds
come to an end every day.

Like waterskiing in a deluge, hitching a ride
on a drop of rain is how the mosquito
survives in a downpour.

Rare event, transit of Venus, when
the planet appears as a small black dot,
a beauty mark penciled on the face of the sun.

Often I would bathe my face with saltwater
from the restless ocean. If there's water on the moon,
it must be frozen by now.

I've yet to see them in flower or bearing fruit,
these sharp brittle twigs, these scratchy
thin branches of the bony thorn-apple tree.

Unseasonably warm, and in the background
of the afternoon press conference, you can hear
mockingbirds on the White House lawn.

Computer graphic art is grooming
virtual hair and feathers of animated
creatures to obey the laws of physics.

You could survive to antiquity and die
alone like hundred-year-old tortoise
just passed away on Galapagos Island.

After official autopsy, carefully preserved
remains of Lonesome George are bubble-wrapped,
duct-taped, and stored in a freezer.

Visiting with you that spring in Maryland,
how often I wished I could gather
those bright cherry blossoms into a tanka!

It wouldn't cost five cents or a nickel
to name as our national mammal
the bison or the American buffalo.

A local ordinance against cruelty
to geese puts an end to foie gras on
a stick wrapped in a cloud of cotton candy.

Pacific pocket mouse—somewhat less
endangered on the firing range where guns
aim at standing targets, not burrowing critters.

You can drive south from San Francisco;
I'll come up from L.A. So let's meet in the middle
at that cheap but cozy beach motel.

Southern California family surprised
to discover uninvited black bear taking
a dip in their suburban pool.

Human footprints in the dust
marked the latest entry in the record
of earth's history written on the surface of the moon.

TUMBLEWEED, name in black letters
on the side of a bright yellow bus
delivering students to open gates of Windward School.

"Who do you think I am? Tippi Hedren
in an Alfred Hitchcock film?" I wondered,
when that flying object pecked me on the head.

So accustomed to minor temblors,
I woke for only a moment before turning
over in bed and going back to sleep.

As you have forgotten, so one day
might you remember how to be wild
and bewildered, to be wilder and be wilderness?

Today's technology allows scientists
to analyze the last meal of a
prehistoric insect preserved in amber.

Craving the season of spring, we hunt for
plump raspberries, fava beans, and pencil-thin
asparagus in the farmers markets.

After all these years, when each has lost
someone we love, you still remember stopping by
to share a meal of lentil soup and bread.

It alters the mood of our calm conversation
when we have to shout to be heard
beneath the roar of jets and helicopters.

Worn by many young women on campus,
casual shorts and sleeveless tops with logo labels
that proclaim them PINK and JUICY.

The ax used to split up the furniture
of her faithless lover, on display
in the museum of broken relationships.

Several homeowners organize a neighbor-
hood watch patrol after discovering used
rubbers discarded on their lawns.

A young man I wouldn't notice, if not for
words overheard, not even whispered
into his phone, "Two-hundred for a blow job."

Intrepid, worldly, and sophisticated food critic
laments she's found no wine pairs well
with scorpions or tarantulas.

While dreaming my way up the mountain,
I sleepwalked into my kitchen
where I slipped on a pebble, or was it a potato?

Hovering half-awake, uncertain if those
sounds were bird or child. We say that human
hatchlings coo, and so do doves and pigeons.

Random genetic tests suggest
the fish brought to your table is unlikely to be
what's written on the restaurant menu.

Later, I wonder if I heard right.
An exceptional hairdresser might have said
to a client, "Two-hundred for a blow-dry."

Rainy, spicy leaves of the California laurel,
scented with a hint of cardamom, like
chewing gum I used to crave.

A student's original excuse for not
turning in her homework—her life turned
inside out by an infestation of bedbugs.

Remember that song about possum in
the 'simmon tree? That's who's living in your
back yard, opossum in the persimmon tree.

Beekeepers couldn't sell the strange green
and blue honey their bees made after
snacking on candy from the M & M factory.

Ha-ha-haw-haw, the dark bird's rowdy laughter
as it flew over the heads of earthbound
pedestrians who didn't get the joke.

In the aftermath of the tsunami,
rescuers look for survivors, find in
the arms of a tree a hungry baby boy.

"But they can't see any ocean from where
they live," the realtor laughs. "That area
could be Mar Vista in English only."

In greening spring when every leafy thing
is waking, the blanched and naked branches
of a gnarled tree look all the more desolate.

"Do you hear me?" Yes, I turn my head.
A stranger talking on the phone, "Listen to me.
Stop saying you're going to kill yourself."

Feeling rueful, seeing the FOR LEASE sign
where their shop used to be. Never went in,
except that one time with the homeless woman.

Unearthed by San Francisco construction workers,
a nugget of gold and a broken ten-inch tooth
of ice age woolly mammoth.

For every community plot and rooftop
garden, how many seeds that sprouted in crooked
cracks, the plants that no one planted?

Zigzag legs, barbed predator claws—startling
discovery, the ancient trogloraptor family
of large cave-dwelling spiders.

With a vigorous push of a broom,
a worker sweeps enterprising squirrel
out the front door of the natural food co-op.

The mockingbird and monarch butterfly
arrive on cue as I sit on a garden bench
to write in the tanka diary.

A scenic backdrop of young bamboo stalks
growing in a corner of the yard, inspiring
the children's tropical adventures.

Versed in country things and sensitive
to seasons, the poet knew that nature never
wept for us no matter how gently it rained.

Favorite sandals, constantly worn,
that remembered the shape of my feet—
lost in a whirlpool as I crossed the roiling water.

I'm sure I must have been laughing
the first time we hiked that mountain trail,
when you introduced me to the sticky monkey flower.

Plain colors we wear, compared to
green-shimmering wings of hummingbird
stroking opulent purple velvet of Mexican sage.

Today we found an ephemeral shrine
at the end of the trail—rocks and pebbles
some hiker had arranged to make a spiral.

In their beach-themed bungalow,
a coffee table built from a recycled
surfboard cut from a California redwood tree.

Halfway across an empty street I pause
to hear water flowing swiftly beneath
where I stand on a sturdy manhole cover.

Even itinerant tumbleweed had roots
attaching it to the land, before its stem snapped
and strong winds pushed it down the road.

Zesty greens tossed with organic virgin
olive oil and vinegar, a salad of weeds
foraged from the pristine countryside.

On a breath of air, they may last longer
and travel farther than we know,
our folded paper boats and origami airplanes.

Caught a quick glimpse of bright eyes,
yellow feathers, dark wings. Never learned your name—
and to you, bird, I also remain anonymous.

III

Uncollected Poems
2001–2021

Liberation of Ms. Liberty

I'm not your doormat any more.
I'm slamming shut my open door.
Keep your tired oppressed and poor.
Wretched refuse, what do I need them for?

Once upon a time, I carried a torch
for foreign-born folks who don't eat with forks.
Now when I see such useless dorks,
I shout, "Hey, loser, stay off my porch!"

I need my own space. There's no room anymore
for freeloaders who think I've got booty galore.
Taking care of your needs is a thankless chore
so just keep off my domestic shores.

It's Not About the Menu

It's not about the menu,
it's about me and you.
You've freed your tastebuds,
they're way ahead,
but your politics are Wonderbread.

You say *olé* to frijoles,
love those tacos and tamales.
My cousin crossed the border today,
and it's "No way, *José*, you can't stay!"

You get take-out sushi,
buy drive-thru teriyaki.
You still can't use me
unless I'm model minority.

You'll try kimchee
and Korean barbecue,
but you don't like me
because I'm not like you.

You eat soul food
any time you're in the mood,
but when I'm in your neighborhood,
you've got a bad attitude.

No time to shop or cook? Don't worry!
Just call for curry in a hurry.
Still you yell at me, a U.S. citizen,
"Go back to wherever you came from!"

Wonton and dim sum,
have it all, and then some.
No matter how successful I am,
no matter how smart,
you're always the main course,
while I'm *à la carte*.

If the spice of life is variety,
why so much strife between you and me?
It's not about the menu, it's about me and you.
If we can savor each other's flavors,
we can thrive together, too.

The Fire This Time

Cave Canem
A poet's retreat
A safe house
A poet's sanctuary

Cave Canem
The poets are dreaming
When a loud noise wakes us
I grab my words and run

Cave Canem
A dog is barking
A fire is starting
The poets are awakened

Cave Canem
The fire is spreading
Detroit's ears are burning
The poets are wide awake

Poetry for Dummies

"Roses often signify love or beauty,
and the worm is often used
to signify death and decay."
O worm, thou art robust and strong.
The garish rose that makes you
act like a prick has shunned you until
you felt like a defunct doornail
signifying decay. Now that she's
caught you lying in her bloody bed,
you'll find that her dark scent
rouses the most rigorous stiff.

Summer Salt

It's no wonder fish fly
when sky's overthrown,
ocean's upended
as blue waves above
capsized clouds,
tropical islands
in airy sea
beneath salty sky
of celestial starfish.

I Want to Thank You, Betye Saar

on the occasion of her 75th birthday

I want to thank you, Betye Saar,
for assembling our torn truths, for collaging
the fragile fragments of our collective history.

I want to thank you, Betye Saar,
for building the gris-gris house
of beautiful black magic.

Thank you, Betye Saar,
for liberating the black Jemimas
who mothered us all.

Thank you, Betye Saar,
for cracking open the slave ship
and giving us passage to ourselves.

Thank you, Betye Saar, for remembering the ancestors
with shrines of dainty gloves and flirtatious fans,
for opening the black girl's window.

Thank you, Betye Saar, mystical digital griot,
for uncovering windows, screens, and mirrors
in which we finally see our secret identities.

Unacknowledged Legislator

After singing the final page
the poet passes out
ceremonial pens.

As the poem is sighed into law
rules to be made are broken
and broken rules amended.

When the archival papers
are all singed in blood
the poet's meter expires.

Bumper to Bumper

I'd rather be at the beach. I'd rather beat each ache. I'd rather be a dirty blond than a clean-cut brunet. If I had to choose between being richer or smarter, I'd rather have the money because I'm smart enough already.

I'd rather not think about it. I'd rather not go into that. I voted but I'd rather not say which one I punched. I'd rather switch than fight. I trust my psychic friend over Dan Rather.

I'm stuck in traffic when I'd rather be surfing. My other car is the Metro, *mi otro carro es El Metro*. I'd rather drive than walk. I'd rather work than starve. I'd rather drink unfiltered tap water and sleep on a lumpy futon than live anywhere else in this godforsaken world.

Headlines

1. Fired cook was deranged.
2. Baldheaded woman's distressed.
3. Flypaper gets inspected.
4. Trial lawyer's profession distorted.
5. Balloonist disgusted, round-the-world trip falls flat.
6. Kiwis, these birds are unflappable.
7. Obese sheep distended.
8. Madonna disguised in convent.
9. Jockey to be debriefed shortly.
10. Las Vegas delighted to conserve power.

#6 Sepulveda

Arrival at terminal laxative. In and out with fries. Fox mauls hill. A colored crowd. Sad cactus left over from family nursery's going out of business sale. The drive-in movie was a used car lot, then a flea market, now it's condos. Botanica across from coffee shop near Cuban restaurant where workers gather for lunch. A few blocks down, you can get five different mole salsas and wire dollars to Oaxaca. At pancake palace I hop on the bus across from all night news guy. Today's special veggie burger at Hot Diggity, home of the Y2K dog. Turn right past blank soldier and bland sailor. A white cross for each life lost. Pencils, toothpicks, chopsticks. Trees in this wood, all cut down to size. Pay a large sum for a large bag of popcorn. End of the line, everyone out. Grab a *Daily Bruin* and run. It's okay, the crazy people on the bus aren't talking to themselves. They're speaking on their cellphones.

Waving the Flag

I'm so deep down in the groove of this hysterical state
called America, I'm completely in step with its patriotic beat:
one drummer drumming, with boots on the ground,
marching, and everybody falling in line.

I promise to be faithful to the flag
that I love so much, I'd marry it.
To wrap its glory around me,
I'd kill or be killed by my enemies.

I pay attention to the fragments
of the disorganized state of my mind,
and to the repossessed souls that cannot understand
one notion of God, with death and destruction for all.

I'm sick of this American kitsch
of the amalgamated mess of love that rich bitch,
and the upholstery on which she sits,
one red-hot, blue-blooded white girl.

I pledge my furniture every week.
I took a vow, and look at me now.
I find myself in a uniform state of loneliness,
with just us hausfraus, that's all.

I guarantee that I'll agree
with every decree from on high—
and any dissenter who disagrees
could be a terrorist, or a spy.

I'm staring up at the mighty flag,
the emblem of war, the symbol of privilege.
I believe in the flag with all my heart, and with all my faith
in the gross national product of the United States of America.

I wave at the flag as the flag waves back.
It whips to and fro in the breeze.
It gives me strength to fight at length,
to whip our enemies and bring them to their knees.

I've got to believe in the bloody flag.
It stands for my country, right or wrong.
I've got to believe in whatever it takes
to keep the nation strong.

I promise to get with the program of patriotic patriarchs.
I'll go with the flow and believe what I'm told.
I'll always obey, whatever they say.
After all, what do I know?

I swear an oath on this tired, wilted banner
that flies from Wisconsin to Alabama.
When my child came home in a bag,
all I got was this bloody rag.

I can't believe they wrote a law to stop crazy artists
and left-wing nuts from peeing
on a burning flag. But I guess it's best
we don't allow such utterly tasteless acts of protest.

Sugar Land

My ancestors raised cane in Sugar Land, Texas. Sugar cane grown on plantations in the Brazos River Bottom, where Stephen F. Austin's Old Three Hundred came to make their fortunes. They smuggled in illegal Africans to work the bitter crop. As long as the planters could get more slaves, who cared how many died—crushed and cut, or moaning with malaria and yellow fever? The first sweetness was unrefined, black molasses so thick you could carry it in a sack. Of course the Texans joined the Confederacy, vowing to lick the Yankees in time to go home for Christmas.

After the war, when Texas prisons took over those plantations, so many men died in convict labor camps, the state closed them down at last. Yet another generation of business-men took charge to make Sugar Land a company town. By then my ancestors had escaped to Freedmen's Town, fleeing the misery of Sugar Land.

Yet they never told us how they raised cane in Sugar Land. Imperial brand sugar I sprinkled on my Cheerios, growing up in Texas.

Documents began to crumble as I unpacked storage boxes at the National Archives. Letters written to and from the Freedmen's Bureau agent in Fort Bend County, Texas: home of Tom Delay and the Jaybird-Woodpecker War. Contracts negotiated between former slaves, now sharecroppers, and former slaveholders who still owned land, houses, barns, livestock, and tools. Those men who had fought as rebels complained that black people wouldn't work hard, insolently free, demanding one day a week to rest and go to church. What planter could profit, paying wages to trifling workers who broke valuable tools, stole horses and mules?

My ancestors raised cane in Sugar Land, Texas. Spoonful of sugar I licked from the top of Ruby Red grapefruit my mother served at Sunday breakfast.

I don't believe they forgot or refused to tell the story. They passed it down in late night tales of Master and John. John, the slave who accidentally set fire to the master's barn.

It was John who somehow lost the master's horse. John even provoked the white man to murder his own grandmother—but only after Master had killed John's grandmother, punishing John for some intolerable crime, like trying to outsmart the slaveholder.

My ancestors raised cane in Sugar Land, Texas. They told tall tales about John and Master, and let me sprinkle Imperial Sugar on my morning bowl of O's.

Curious Strangers

My grandfather Lowell was a native son
returning to Texas,
but his young wife and daughter
had never lived south
of the Mason-Dixie.
Friends, neighbors, and church members
stepped up to help the pastor's family
adjust to their new home.
They advised my grandmother
on avoiding discomfort and danger
while driving, dining, shopping,
and attending to any business
that involved white people.

On a particular summer day,
as my mother Avis and my grandmother Harryette
were shopping in downtown Fort Worth,
a succession of strangers approached them to ask,
"How come y'all ain't at the barbecue?"
After several puzzled and polite
"I beg your pardons" from my grandmother,
one stranger finally explained, it was
the nineteenth of June, a holiday for black folk.

Only then did my grandmother and mother realize
they were the only black people in sight.
That was why they'd attracted
the attention of curious strangers.

Some families celebrated Juneteenth in backyards
or neighborhood parks, while many attended a huge picnic
with free barbecue from Armour and Swift,
meat packing plants that had drawn black workers
to the end of the cattle trail, also known as Cow Town.

Born in Harrisburg, Pennsylvania, where
they attended Watch Night at church on New Year's Eve,
observing Emancipation Day on the first of January,
my mother and grandmother knew nothing of Juneteenth,
the summer Jubilee when black Texans celebrated freedom—
however delayed by Lone Star rebels who fought on,
months after General Lee's surrender.

Remove Offensive Language

Yes, it's true that numerous people
(perhaps including a handful of liars,
murderers, thieves, and blasphemers)
bear the name of the honorable bleep.

(May he rest in eternal peace.)

Yet one must be careful how,
when, where, and to whom one speaks
the exalted name of bleep.

No image can exist of him
whose precious name is bleep,
so no one has any bleeping idea
what the bleep he looks like.

Still it is forbidden
to create any copy or likeness
to represent the unimaginable
facc of bleep.

Just as it is forbidden to sully
with thought, deed, or word
the most perfect and impeccable
name of bleep.

"Blue herons persist"
(from Renga for Obama*)*

Blue herons persist
in riparian thickets
along Potomac.

Barbaracrostics
(Racing through Theory)

Black body
Academic alien
Reigning reactionary
Biological blueprint
Attack Africa
Repeating repressive
Authority appalled

Black books
Artist ally
Radical resisted
Break binary
Affirmation articulated
Radical reclamation
Another approach

Coopted critics
Humanists hegemony
Repulsive reason
Institutions infiltrated
Social stereotyping
Theory takeover
Ignore insight
Abstract assault
Narrowness narratives

Celebrated creating
Hidden hieroglyphs
Reading riddles
Imagine intersection
Sensual spiritedness
Theorizing today
Ideas influenced
Activity accelerates
Necessary nourishment

Y the Or

Y the or, why
You or I
Yes or no
In or out
Pro or con
Hero or zero
The Y or X
Female or male, or other
Black or white, or other
The one or the other
Left or right
Life or choice
Able or unable
Legal or illegal
Fake or real
Rich or poor, wealthy or not
Paper or plastic
Half full or half empty
It's true or it's false
I agree or I disagree
I will or I won't
My freedom or your freedom
Or fork in the road of Y or Y not

IV

Critical Essays

Every Difference Contains a Difference Within It: Harryette Mullen's Earlier and Later Poetry

Alan Gilbert

Harryette Mullen's two most recently published books of poetry demonstrate differing approaches to identity, ethnicity, and multiculturalism. The first is entitled *Blues Baby: Early Poems* (2002), which reprints her first book, *Tree Tall Woman*, from 1981, along with a selection of uncollected early poems. The second is *Sleeping with the Dictionary* (2002a). The changes in Mullen's poetry—in terms of form and content—should immediately be obvious to most readers of the two books. *Blues Baby* is in many respects a more "conventional" book of poems than *Sleeping with the Dictionary*, whether this applies to the form of individual poems or the structure of the book as a whole. But instead of using these books to argue for a fixed progression in Mullen's poetics, or what upon cursory inspection seems to be an increasing sophistication in her poetic practice, it may be more useful to evaluate the differing formal strategies and ideological concerns contained in each.

For years after her embrace of and by avant-garde poets and poetics associated with the Language poetry movement, Mullen distanced herself from the poems in *Tree Tall Woman* as being too essentialist in their understanding of race and ethnicity, too un-self-reflexive in their presentation of a unified lyric "I," and too conventional in poetic form.[1] The interesting question, then, is why Mullen has decided at

413

this particular moment in time—both in relation to her own writing career and, perhaps more importantly, in relation to aesthetic and political debates within the poetry world and outside of it—to republish this earlier work. I'd argue that her decision reflects a complex understanding of what it means to be concerned with issues of identity and multiculturalism at the beginning of the twenty-first century, and is part of an attempt to reconceive notions of difference.

One way of metaphorically articulating this is to say that every difference contains a difference within it. The near simultaneous publication of *Blues Baby* and *Sleeping with the Dictionary*, despite being written nearly twenty years apart, is meant to throw into question easy assumptions about difference. Their publication indicates Mullen's awareness of differences within the same communities, within individuals, and within a single body of work. Of course, if one remains committed to this notion of difference, then one should not immediately assume which audience will be associated with which book, i.e., that a reader not familiar with postmodern poetics will be the primary reader of *Blues Baby* and that the opposite will be the case with *Sleeping with the Dictionary*, or, more to the point, that one is necessarily a more "advanced" or "radical" text than the other. People use a wide variety of cultural products, avant-garde or not, in order to effect both resistances to and complicities with dominant cultures and ideologies.

Though she frequently talks about the avant-garde formal techniques she's employed in books that come after the poems included in *Blues Baby*, Mullen also continues to raise the issue of marginal communities, thereby connecting linguistic practices with social formations. More recently, Mullen has reversed this relationship and talked about the traditions of innovation that arise within marginal communities, which is not the same as cultural workers from marginal communities utilizing avant-garde techniques: "I don't think there's an automatic linkage between being marginalized or oppressed and being innovative, but I do think that being oppressed does call upon all of your resources, and often out of that comes innovation."[2] In regards to Mullen's work, innovation is usually associated by her and scholars of her writing with white, European avant-garde techniques (specifically those employed by Gertrude Stein in *Tender Buttons* [1962] and by the writers constituting the group known as Oulipo;[3] however, expanding on the idea of innovation within marginalization, Mullen also stresses the importance for her work of a black tradition of "vernacular innovation."[4]

Black feminists were among the first to formulate the theory of differences within differences, primarily in response to what they experienced as the predominantly white, middle-class quality of 1970s mainstream feminism. The poems in *Blues Baby* are written in the wake of this challenge. They deal, as poetry is well suited to do, with issues of representation: representations of self and representations of black people within and outside of their communities. In fact, along with drawing from a tradition of "vernacular innovation," Mullen's challenge to the image- and identity-shaping powers of representation has remained her most consistent theme over the course of twenty years of published work. Obviously, the two are closely related, as the vernacular takes dominant languages, images, and cultural forms and creatively—and oftentimes subversively—adapts them to the specific sets of historical conditions facing oppressed, exploited, and marginalized groups.

Whatever formal techniques Mullen employs, these issues of representation have remained central to her work. This entails subverting existing representations and creating new ones. In *Blues Baby*, the means for undermining pernicious representations of black individuals and communities in mainstream U.S. culture is to create positive ones, particularly of the everyday life of black women. In doing so, she taps into: "[T]he dominant black art tradition of figuration, ever popular because it is the most effective vehicle for correcting the long history of visual caricatures of black people."[5] At the same time, Mullen does not shy away from depicting the hardships black women face, whether inside or outside their own communities. Hence, the importance in *Blues Baby* of describing a place of real or imagined safety, as in the poem "Circle of Arms."[6] In Mullen's poetry, this sense of safety is distinguished by its transience, partly because Mullen rarely locates it in either family or traditional black institutions such as the church, unless in fleetingly imagined or remembered forms, as in the opening poems of *Blues Baby* in which Mullen recalls moments from her childhood and reminisces about absent relatives. Rather, safety is temporarily found in friendships and intimate relationships with members of both sexes. Though significant and meaningful while occurring, not all of these intense relations are enduring.

This sense of love gone wrong and friendships betrayed is very much in keeping with blues traditions. So, too, is the way in which the experiences of a single person—either the blues artist or the personas presented in the blues artist's songs—metonymically represent the collective experiences of entire communities. This is one way of understanding the fluid eroticism and sexuality of *Blues Baby*, with its title implying that the poems therein are partially engendered by blues traditions. In her study of Gertrude "Ma" Rainey, Bessie Smith, and Billie Holiday, Angela Davis outlines this connection between female blues singers, the explicit sexuality of their lyrics, and black communities: "Sexuality is not privatized in the blues. Rather, it is represented as shared experience that is socially produced";[7] furthermore, the blues signify: "[T]he tradition of representing love and sexuality as both concrete daily experience and as coded yearning for social liberation."[8] *Blues Baby* contains a number of poems in which Mullen attempts to write and revise traditional blues lyrics:

> The Joy
> Here's a bowl of batter
> for your spoon to stir.
> Here's an oven
> to bake your bread in.
> Put some starch
> in your chef's hat, honey,
> and start cookin. (2002: 53)

In these and many other poems in the book, Mullen expresses a sense of emptiness seeking to be filled. This literal and figurative hunger is both individual and collective, and it affirms Davis' notion that the blues blur the boundaries between private and communal life.

The ability to fashion a persona in the blues is crucial to understanding how expressions of self and identity function in a complicated manner in *Blues Baby*. If one of the primary directives of minority and feminist literatures in the 1970s and 1980s was to "find your voice" and to not be silenced, Mullen articulated rather early in her work the understanding that voice is not synonymous with self. *Blues Baby* is filled with examples of this: from poems explicitly written from a man's point of view,[9] to three poems written from the perspective of the mythological siren as well as the victims of her song,[10] to poems that use mirrors to question self-identity,[11] to poems that playfully and self-consciously adopt a blues woman's style and attitude.[12] Interestingly, the majority of these poems were not published in *Tree Tall Woman*, but are ones Mullen chose to accompany its new edition. As a result, *Blues Baby* juxtaposes the budding coming-of-age/coming-to-consciousness subjectivity in *Tree Tall Woman* with a more mature identity that's frequently called into question in the uncollected early poems that constitute the second half of the book.

One poem in *Tree Tall Woman* that deals with a number of these issues and anticipates future directions Mullen's work would take is "He Reads My Body Like a Poem":

He reads my body like a poem.
My skin has lines of bad grammar,
but he recites it with a straight face.
He is serious and uses no rhyme.

I laugh at the limerick I am—
"eyes" rhymed with "thighs,"
"tits" with "armpits."

I know this poet,
unflappable performer,

could ad-lib from
a book of empty pages.[13]

The idea of the female body as a revolutionary written text was shared by U.S. feminists and French poststructuralist feminists alike, sometimes contemporaneously, as in the theory of écriture féminine. But the written-upon-body has less positive connotations, as when the body becomes the place where power leaves its most immediate inscriptions, or, even more concretely, when the body becomes the site where women contest their rights to self-determination in struggles over abortion, health care, and representations of the female body in fashion and mass media. Summing up the thinking at the time, Teresa de Lauretis wrote: "The stakes, for women, are rooted in the body—which is not to say that the body escapes representation, but quite the opposite."[14] In general, minority women have had an even greater struggle in this regard, as their attempts to obtain direct access to legal rights, health care, and depictions of themselves in the media are constantly frustrated.

Mullen combines all of these concerns in her poem, while ultimately promoting the power of poetry, play, and the eroticized body. Ambiguities pervade the poem, beginning right away with the title and first line. What does it mean to read a "body like a poem"? How does this differ from other modes of reading? It appears that reading a body like a poem creates the potential for a more liberated kind of reading, one that entails a certain amount of give-and-take. At the same time, relations of power are immediately invoked by the fact that this is a man reading a woman's body, however dialogic this reading may be. The reference to "bad grammar" in the second line indicates both an internalization of negative representations of minority women in U.S. society, while also referencing the innovative vernacular traditions Mullen employs against these negative stereotypes. In this sense, "bad grammar" connotes playfulness and the imaginative ways in which minority groups adapt "standard English" to their own material circumstances and cultural traditions. But

the male reader—and the societal forces it is possible to read him as embodying—reads her body seriously, perhaps in an attempt to contain its potential for alternative racialized and gendered modes of representation and interpretation. An argument might even be made that the combination of the phrase "bad grammar" (a linguistic trait that has a history of being ascribed by the ruling orders to the lower ones)[15] with the mentioning of laughter, limerick, and sexualized and sometimes "dirty" body parts in the next stanza generates more than a hint of the carnivalesque body threatening to upset social hierarchies.[16]

Thus, in the second stanza, the "I" contests the male reader's/lover's seriousness by laughing and by rhyming in the face of the "he" who neither laughs nor rhymes. Yet the "bad grammar" she initially embraces is suddenly tempered by a set of fairly conventional direct rhymes. The struggle continues over whose text her body is and how that text is to be read. The second stanza also reveals how different their ideas about her body are: she sees her body as playful, rhyming, and erotic (one almost immediately associates the limerick form with bawdy content, which is reinforced by Mullen's rhyme of "'tits' with 'armpits'"); he sees her body as serious, non-rhyming, and may prefer reading to less cerebral passions. "[E]fforts to control Black women's sexuality lie at the heart of Black women's oppression," writes Patricia Hill Collins (2000: 81), though just as important are efforts to control their labor. He may also be, as Mullen writes elsewhere in *Blues Baby*, one of the men who want to carry away the song (2002: 34). He does seem to want to carry away a certain kind of song that she represents, or represents to herself, or is represented by others. It's never quite clear, which is appropriate, given how knotted an issue representation is, particularly representations of women, and especially representations of minority women.

Of course, the poem functions as a commentary on the relationship between critics and texts. However, this meta-critical angle embedded in "He Reads My Body Like a Poem" is secondary to the larger issues of how the bodies of minority women are controlled by and rebel against both symbolic representations and material conditions. The confident assertion at the beginning of the third stanza—"I know this poet"—reaffirms the woman's understanding of the situation and its variety of power relations (and the possibility for their dismantling), an awareness that once again changes the tone of the poem. She also seems slightly in awe of his linguistic capacities in a way that first and foremost connotes respect for him and the poetic and cultural traditions he symbolizes, but, like so much in this apparently simple and formally conventional poem, is filled with conflict and uncertainty. His mastery (his "unflappable" nature, his ability to "ad-lib" on the spot), however much admired, causes her to introduce *Blues Baby*'s ongoing theme of emptiness, moving from her body as a rich text to "a book of empty pages."

The many levels at which this poem operates, and which I've really only glanced upon—from gendered interpersonal relations, to self-reflexive textuality, to cultural transmissions within black communities, to the relationship of these communities (and particularly the women in them) to a patriarchal and racist U.S. society—illuminate the multifaceted dimensions of Mullen's early poetry. Mullen's appreciation of differences within differences, and the diverse writing and cultural communities with which she is affiliated, need to be taken into account when thinking about her decision to republish this earlier work alongside *Sleeping with the Dictionary*.

In a poem from *Tree Tall Woman* in *Blues Baby* entitled "Playing the Invisible Saxophone en el Combo de las Estrellas," Mullen declares that:

> One of these days I'm gonna write a real performance poem.
> [. . .]
> a get-down poem so kinetically energetic
> it sure put disco to shame.
> Make it a snazzy jazzy poem extravaganza, with pizzazz.
> Poem be going solo,
> flying high on improbable improvisational innovation.
> Poem be blowing hard![17]

And in an uncollected poem near the end of *Blues Baby*, the last thing she hears before she leaves a Greyhound bus station is: "A kid doing an avant-garde / improvisational number".[18] Mullen's published works after *Tree Tall Woman* and the other early poems in *Blues Baby* have all aspired to and in places have marvelously and masterfully achieved this improvisational quality. In the process, the form and some of the concerns of her work have changed. After the free-verse poems in *Blues Baby*, her next three books were written more loosely, though within relatively strict formal constraints: the short prose blocks of *Trimmings* (1991) and *S*PeRM**K*T* (1992), whose title can be read as both "supermarket" and "spermkit," and the short-lined quatrains of *Muse & Drudge* (1995). Yet within these determining structures, Mullen creates a space to freely improvise and address a range of issues either briefly touched on or not addressed at all in the poems contained in *Blues Baby*. The significant differences between the poems in *Blues Baby* and the later *Trimmings* and *S*PeRM**K*T*, and between those two books and the recent *Sleeping with the Dictionary*, reveal a writer who has consistently reevaluated her literary and intellectual practice within changing personal, aesthetic, and political circumstances.

Moreover, Mullen began to recognize the importance of expectations and writing a certain way when it came to composing work that would bring her different audiences together.[19] Obviously, these audiences do not congregate spontaneously; rather, they are dependent upon a set of institutional structures—however informal these may sometimes be—and fields of cultural production for their experience of poetry (or any cultural product, for that matter). And with institutions and fields of cultural production come expected formal methods, discursive modes, cultural styles, personal behaviors, and governing ideologies. Beginning with *Muse & Drudge* and more fully in *Sleeping with the Dictionary*, Mullen's work has subtly shifted away from a poetics of language in itself—and language about language—to a more vernacular, organic, and less predetermined sense of innovation.

In certain ways, this has brought her most recent work a little closer to the poems in *Blues Baby*, but with the substantial kinds of differences personal and collective histories always accrue.

Notes

1. Griffin, Farah, Magee, Michael, and Gallagher, Kristen (1999) "A Conversation with Harryette Mullen." Electronic Poetry Center website. http://wings.buffalo.edu/epc/authors/mullen /interview-new.html. n.p.; Harryette Mullen, "Poetry and Identity." In *West Coast Line*. No. 19, Vol. 30, No. 1 (Spring 1996): 85–89.
2. Mullen, Harryette, Untitled. In *Tripwire*. Special issue: "Expanding the Repertoire: Continuity and Change in African-American Writing," eds. Yedda Morrison and David Buuck. No. 5 (Fall 2001): 11–14.
3. Mathews, Harry, and Brotchie, Alastair, eds. (1998) *Oulipo Compendium*. Atlas Press, London. Motte, Jr., Warren F., ed. (1998) *Oulipo: A Primer of Potential Literature*. Dalkey Archive Press, Normal, IL.
4. Mullen, Harryette, Untitled. In *Tripwire*, 12; "Imagining the Unimagined Reader: Writing to the Unborn and Including the Excluded." In *boundary 2*. Special issue: "99 Poets/1999: An International Poetics Symposium," ed. Charles Bernstein. Vol. 26, No. 1 (Spring 1999): 198–203. 201–202.
5. Ross, Andrew (2002) "Golden Moment." In *Artforum*. Vol. 40, No. 8 (April 2002): 27–28. 27.
6. Mullen, Harryette (2002a) *Sleeping with the Dictionary*. University of California Press, Berkeley and Los Angeles, 78.
7. Davis, Angela Y. (1998) *Blues Legacies and Black Feminism: Gertrude "Ma" Rainey, Bessie Smith, and Billie Holiday*. Vintage Books, New York, 91.
8. Davis, *Blues Legacies*, 173.
9. Harryette Mullen (2002) *Blues Baby: Early Poems*. Bucknell University Press, Lewisburg, PA; Associated University Presses, London, 97, 105.
10. Mullen, *Blues Baby*, 132, 133, 134.
11. Mullen, *Blues Baby*, 79–80, 127–128.

12. Mullen, *Blues Baby*, 53, 86–88, 90, 93, 104, 105, 106, 120, 122.

13. Mullen, *Blues Baby*, 61.

14. de Lauretis, Teresa (1986) "Feminist Studies/Critical Studies: Issues, Terms, and Contexts." In *Feminist Studies/Critical Studies*, ed. Teresa de Lauretis. Indiana University Press, Bloomington, 1–19. 12.

15. Smith, Olivia (1984) *The Politics of Language, 1791–1819*. Clarendon Press, Oxford.

16. Bakhtin, Mikhail (1984) *Rabelais and His World*. Trans. Helene Iswolsky. Indiana University Press, Bloomington; Stallybrass, Peter, and White, Allon (1986) *The Politics and Poetics of Transgression*. Cornell University Press, Ithaca, NY.

17. Mullen, *Blues Baby*, 68.

18. Mullen, *Blues Baby*, 137.

19. Griffin, "A Conversation with Harryette Mullen," n.p.; Mullen, Untitled. In *Tripwire*, 13; Mullen, "Poetry and Identity," 88.

On Being Amused: Harryette Mullen's *Muse & Drudge*

Emily Greenwood

Introducing her threefold poetry collection *Recyclopedia*, published in 2006, Harryette Mullen remarked, 'I have written all of these works from my perspective as a black woman, which I believe is no less representative of humanity than any other point of view.'[1] No less representative, but traditionally under-represented as writer, artist, and intellectual, hence Mullen's recourse to a rhetorical negative ('no less . . .') to gainsay Western humanism. Mullen's reinvention of the classical figure of the muse in her 1995 collection *Muse & Drudge*, reprinted as the third movement of *Recyclopedia*, exploits this ambivalence as Mullen explores the condition of being un-mused or a-mused, bracketed off within an aesthetic tradition of which one is manifestly a part.[2] Mullen's muse is amused in her propensity for all manner of word play, and she is simultaneously *a*-mused through misrecognition—the muse mistaken for drudge. At the heart of Mullen's collection is the paradox of recognizing oneself unimagined and of writing up from under prevailing stereotypes. At the same time, Mullen's complex, innovative, experimental poetics challenges readers to recognize what Nathaniel Mackey has called 'black artistic othering', converting the object status of being the other to the subject status of othering or re-versioning the tradition.[3] This goes to the heart of Mullen's articulation of an original theory of black reader-response criticism: 'When I read words never meant for me, or anyone like me—words that exclude me, or anyone like me, as a possible reader—then I feel simultaneously my exclusion and my inclusion as a literate black woman, the unimagined reader of the text.'[4]

Mae Gwendolyn Henderson has adapted the trope of 'speaking in tongues' to encapsulate the interlocutory plays that structure the discourse of black women writers.[5] By interweaving classical tropes and fragments into a 'creative dialogue' which is characterised by the presence of several simultaneous discourses and intersecting identities, Harryette Mullen poses insistent questions about adaptation and proprietary use that reflect long-running debates about the interdependence of the aesthetic and the social in black poetics.[6] Mullen's articulation of a theory of authorship based around the figure of the unimagined reader anticipates Sara Ahmed's conception of use in *What's the Use? On the Uses of Use*.[7] Reflecting on the multiple ways in which notions of proper use are used to discriminate between in- and out-groups, Sara Ahmed describes a politics of 'queer use', explaining that 'Queer use might refer to how things can be used in ways other than they were intended to be used or by those other than for whom they were intended' (44). Even more pertinent for Mullen's poetic practice in *Muse & Drudge* is Ahmed's suggestion that 'queer use provides [us] with a way of making connections between histories that might otherwise be assumed to be apart' (198).

Muse & Drudge starts with a shadowy evocation of Sappho that is at once catachresis—creative misuse—and bi-translation: 'Sapphire's lyre styles. . . .'[8] As Diana Fuss has cautioned, the literary analysis of allusion in African American literature must be alert to the process of 'bi-translation', translation across and within two different traditions simultaneously.[9] Mullen has commented on this duality: '*Muse & Drudge* is, on the one hand, a pretty straightforward praise song to women of the African diaspora, although a good deal of it is less than flattering; on the other hand, it is a blues riff on Sappho as Sapphire' (where Sapphire is a derogatory term for a sexualized black woman).[10] Readers of Audre

Lorde may remember that 'Sapphire Sapphos' is the name of a black lesbian social, cultural, and political group founded in Washington DC in 1979. In a diary entry for January 15, 1984, first published in *A Burst of Light*, Lorde mentions being hosted by the Sapphire Sapphos on a reading tour of Washington DC:

> I've just returned from three days in Washington D.C. It was an extraordinary reading. The second evening spent with the Sapphire Sapphos was like 2001 *Space Odyssey* time—the past dreaming the future blooming real and tasty into the present, now.[11]

Tracing the black womanist tradition back through Lorde, we find Sapphire included in the catalogue of the disrespect paid to black women in *The Combahee River Collective* statement of 1977:

> Merely naming the performative stereotype attributed to Black women (e.g. mammy, matriarch, Sapphire, whore, bulldagger), let alone cataloguing the cruel, often murderous, treatment we receive, indicates how little value has been placed upon our lives during four centuries of bondage in the Western hemisphere [. . .] We reject pedestals, queenhood, and walking ten paces behind. To be recognized as human, levelly human, is enough.[12]

Muse & Drudge explores the speculative possibilities of signifying along the spectrum of constraint between 'pedestals' and 'walking ten paces behind.'[13] As Fannie Lou Hamer mused with her audience in a memorable speech in Lexington Mississippi on May 8, 1969, ten paces behind could be figured as counter-intuitive, strategic grounds for civil rights activism: 'And I can challenge any white man anywhere on the face of this earth because God knows he made a mistake when he put me behind. I watched him, now I know him; he doesn't know me.'[14] This is the other dimension of Mullen's title: in the phrase *Muse & Drudge*, the noun 'drudge' activates the graphic and sonic pun of 'Muse' and 'Mule,' evoking the statement, voiced by the character Nanny in Zora Neale Hurston's novel *Their Eyes Were Watching God*, that 'De Nigger Women is De Mule uh de World so far as Ah can see.'[15] To underscore this signifying, Mullen uses the phrase 'Muse of the world' on p. 115.[16] This word play on muse and mule tightens the conjunction in Mullen's title, creating a compound persona. Contiguity with the drudge and the verbal echo of the mule endows the muse with a certain undercommons sensibility.[17] As Joshua Bennett has argued in a reappraisal of the figure of the mule in Hurston's novel,

> Though Hurston certainly returns to the mule repeatedly as a site of unspoken and unspeakable violence, there are also other moments in the novel when it becomes clear that Hurston is interested in the mule as a site of political possibility, of radical imagination set free by misrecognition.[18]

In her choice of epigraph for the collection, Mullen traces a warped line of descent from Greek epic, citing the epic invocation of the muse, but in Callimachus' revisionist version: 'Fatten your animal for sacrifice, poet | but keep your muse slender' (Callimachus *Aetia* fragment 1 [response to the Telchines], lines 23–24, quoted in Diane Rayor's translation).[19] This is a complex classical invocation, since this is one of the most famous instances of *recusatio*, a programmatic refusal to write a particular kind of poem or to follow the conventions of a poetic genre. In this case, Callimachus rejects grand themes of epic in pursuit of a self-proclaimed minor poetics. Mullen borrows Callimachus' *recusatio* only to reversion it with black feminist difference, rejecting the constraints of the 'slender muse'. Evie Shockley has interpreted Mullen's citation of Callimachus as a template for an 'African American Blues Epic' composed, serially, of the 'kinky lyric quatrains of the blues tradition.'[20] In an interview with Nibir Ghosh in 2005, Mullen explained that she wanted to use Callimachus' play on the economy of different poetic genres to cue her readers into a book-length collection of short prose lyric poems, while also hinting at the politicized aesthetics of black women's bodies:

> Taken out of its original context [. . .] and placed in rela-
> tion to this work about people of color, especially African
> American women, the quote can be read as a comment on
> contemporary discussions of physical beauty, body image,
> health, obesity, dieting, and eating disorders. The epigraph
> also highlights the oppositional images of earthy versus ethe-
> real women to which my title refers.[21]

Mullen locates her work in the chain of translation, adapting
Sappho through the mediation of Diane Rayor's translation,
'Diane Rayor had translated surviving fragments of Sappho's
ancient Greek poetry into an American idiom that sounded
to my ear like a woman singing the blues.'[22] There is nothing
incidental or recessive about the work of translation here.
As Mullen has pointed out, the first two words of the collec-
tion, 'Sapphire's Lyre,' adapt the title of Rayor's translation
of Greek lyric poetry, *Sappho's Lyre* through homophonic
translation.[23] The translational logic of *Muse & Drudge*
has become even more explicit since its initial publication
in 1995 as it now forms part of a larger project that Mullen
has conceptualized as a *Recyclopedia*, the title of the 2006
collection in which *Muse & Drudge* was reprinted with the
earlier works *Trimmings* (1991) and *S*PeRM**K*T* (1992).
Explaining the logic of the collection, Mullen coins the
concept of the 'recyclopedia':

> If the encyclopedia collects general knowledge, the recyclo-
> pedia salvages and finds imaginative uses for knowledge.
> That's what poetry does when it remakes and renews words,
> images, and ideas, transforming surplus cultural information
> into something unexpected.[24]

Mullen's recyclopedia presents a postmodern practice of
adaptation. Lisa Mansell has associated the poetics of recy-
cling with sampling in music: 'Each cliché or idiom and
slogan is defamiliarised by blending with a different concep-
tual metaphor or context, by subverting it from the original
ever so subtly – a copy of a copy of a copy.'[25] The first poem
in the *Muse & Drudge* collection encapsulates the experience

of both bi-translation and divergent reading.[26] The verse form
is the quatrain and each page-poem in the collection com-
prises four of these stanzas:

Sapphire's lyre styles
plucked eyebrows
bow lips and legs
whose lives are lovely too

My last nerve's lucid music
sure chewed up the juicy fruit
you must don't like my peaches
there's some left on the tree

You've had my thrills
a reefer tub of gin
don't mess with me I'm evil
I'm in your sin

clipped bird eclipsed moon
soon no memory of you
no drive or desire survives
you flutter invisible still

The first two stanzas of this poem have received close critical
attention.[27] The critic Marjorie Perloff has analyzed Mullen's
use of language in this collection as 'paragrammatical,' drift-
ing in and out of strict grammatical and syntactical sense.[28]
Matthew Hart extends this insight, suggesting that, in '*Muse
& Drudge*, conflicting linguistic fields are enjambed so as to
reveal the shared but unequal history that remains embed-
ded in words and phrases.'[29] For Anthony Reed the shift-
ing, paragrammatic quality of Mullen's lyric suggests 'blues
irony': 'Repetition and citation are techniques of what I'm
calling blues irony: the interruption of one discourse with
a(n) abrupt shift of register or unmotivated repetition that
reorganises the hermeneutic coordinates of a text.'[30] This
interruption already occurs in the first word of the poem (and
of the entire collection), where Sappho mutates into Sapphire.
Fragments of Sappho are then present under erasure, as they

yield to commonplaces from the blues tradition. As Juliana Spahr has discussed, the lines,

> you must don't like my peaches
> there's some left on the tree

allude to Sappho fragment 105a, apparently part of a wedding song (*epithalamium*), where the image of a lofty apple seems to have been used as a canny comparison for a bride.[31] Mullen worked with Diane Rayor's translation of this fragment (Rayor, *Sappho's Lyre*, 74):

> The sweet apple reddens on a high branch
> High upon the highest, missed by the applepickers:
> No, they didn't miss, so much as couldn't touch

In Mullen's version a blues riff covers the quotation; 'peach' has been substituted for the quince apple of Sappho's fragment. The riff starts a flow of allusion within popular American culture, as these lines echo different blues singers, many of whom improvised different versions of the lines. Depending on the reader's knowledge of the tradition, the lines may suggest *Mama's Got the Blues*, recorded by Bessie Smith: 'if you don't like my peaches, please let my orchard be,'[32] Blind Lemon Jefferson's 'Peach Orchard Mama', Ella Fitzgerald's rendition of 'St. Louis Blues', or a common Blues trope. It is the very tradition of blues improvisation which Mullen recycles here. In addition to its resonances for an American target audience, where it evokes an allusive blues complex of sexual puns, Mullen's substitution of 'peaches' for the conventional translation of 'apple' also rhymes with a probable sexual pun in Sappho's Greek.[33] The Blues references in the opening quatrains are interspersed with Jazz references and references to popular culture. As Elisabeth Frost notes, Mullen cues in Billy Strayhorn's Jazz classic 'Lush Life' alongside Rudy Greene's rock and roll song 'Juicy Fruit,' simultaneously name-checking one of the nation's most recognizable brands of chewing gum.[34] Lisa Mansell puts it best, describing 'the collision of languid, bluesy quatrains and

jumpy hot-jazz fragments.'[35] This recycling is offset by con-
stant verbal experimentation, as Mullen adapts and subverts
familiar lines and idioms. As Mark Scroggins has observed,
'Mullen delights in gesturing at but narrowly missing the
expected phrase. One looks twice at "you've had my thrills"
to make sure she hasn't written the lifeless "you've had your
thrills."'[36]

The complex play of translation is underscored by
Mullen's choice of cover art for the first edition of the col-
lection, featuring a photograph of a black woman attending
a public hearing, captured in a posture that is suggestive of a
soulful gospel singer or blueswoman.[37] Even before opening
the cover of *Muse & Drudge*, readers are implicated in the
visual politics of viewing and reading black women. As Farah
Jasmine Griffin has explored in a seminal article, the figure
of the spectacle of the singing black woman is commonly
exploited in majority American culture; while notionally a
muse, she is one whose performance 'serves the unit, who
heals and nurtures it, but has no rights of privileges within
it—more mammy than mother.'[38] The fact that the woman
featured on the cover is apt to be mistaken for a singer when
she is in fact pictured in the process of exercising citizenship
makes Griffin's argument all the more salient for interpreting
Mullen's choice of cover art (see Figure 2).

The visual ambiguity in the choice of cover art sets up the
complex play of identity and representation that will inform
every aspect of the collection, including the question of what
it means to write as a black woman poet. The bi-translation
of the title and the paratextual cover art frames the multi-
directional practice of translation within the work itself,
where Mullen's syncretic poetics models divergent commu-
nities of readers and modes of textual experience, without
reconciling them. When Mullen writes the quatrain,[39]

> you can sing their songs
> with words your way
> put it over to the people
> know what you are doing

Front cover of the 1995 edition of *Muse & Drudge* (Singing Horse Press)

We can read the poet's voice as alluding to Horace's advice to would-be poets in the *Ars Poetica*, where 'their songs' are the Greek models that the Roman poet must appropriate and adapt for his own literary works, and 'your way' is an idiom attuned to Roman, vernacular culture.[40] In Mullen's re-versioning 'their songs' encompasses Sappho, Horace, and other Greek and Roman 'classics' and 'your way' a domesticating strategy of adaptation for an omni-American target culture; but we can also read 'their songs' as the songs of the blues tradition, Jazz standards, hip-hop, and of vernacular culture—including nursery songs and advertising jingles—which Mullen is able to appropriate for her own poetic idiom ('your way') in pursuit of formal innovation and complex intertextual dialogues. The phrase 'put it over to the people' seems to suggest the vernacular contract between the African American artist and their audience developed in Ralph Ellison's famous essay, 'The Little Man at Chehaw Station' (1978). Ellison's little man enjoys the 'confounding of hierarchical expectations,' has an instinct for 'cultural incongruity,' and is able to 'temper the chilliest of classics to his own vernacular taste.'[41] But for Mullen, no less than Ellison, the result is a synthetic vernacular.[42] Mullen's canny signifying derives authority for this remixing from both classical and vernacular tropes of adaptation.[43]

Underpinning this multi-directional translation practice is Mullen's commitment to formal innovation in the tradition of language poetry, given fullest expression in *Sleeping with the Dictionary* (2002), which summons the lexicographical archive to penetrate 'the denotative body of the work' (p. 67), taking on what Christina Sharpe would later term both the 'orthography' and the 'dysgraphia' of the wake.[44] As Mullen's choice of the erotic metaphor 'sleeping with the dictionary' indicates, this project is also kindred with Marlene NourbeSe Philip's poetic theorization of a black womanist philological poetics: how do you love (*philein* in ancient Greek) a language that has been and continues to be expressive of your non-being?[45]

Sappho's fragmentary corpus offers women authors a more suggestive 'denotative body' than other extant Greek classics. Susan Gubar has likened Sappho to the 'fantasy precursor' who represents 'all the lost women of genius in literary history,' adding, 'precisely because so many of her original Greek poems were destroyed, the modern woman poet could write "for" or "as" Sappho and thereby invent a classical inheritance of her own.'[46] Black women authors have developed a distinctive tradition of receiving Sappho, where the double eccentricity of black womanhood encounters the already eccentric Sappho of the classical tradition, bio-fictions and all.[47] For the kind of satirical, postmodern troping of Sappho that Mullen gives us, the closest example is Fran Ross' *Oreo* (1974), released in a new edition in 2000 with a foreword by Mullen. Oreo, the titular character, is an Afro-Jewish girl who starts the novel as Christine, but whose family give her the nickname Oriole; the neighbors then unkindly twist this to Oreo—a girl who is black on the outside and white on the inside. Ostensibly *Oreo*'s classical model is the myth of Theseus. Helen of Troy belongs to a segment of Theseus' life that Ross chooses not to narrate, but in her mythological key at the end of the novel she flags them up as surplus mythological material, possibly available for her heroine's extratextual future: 'Further adventures of the Hero: Theseus and the Amazons; Theseus and Phaedra and Hippolytus; Theseus and Pereithous and Helen and Hades.'[48] Nevertheless, Helen of Troy makes it into the novel in the character of Oreo's mother, Helen. Like Helen of Troy, this Helen is serially absent. In chapter 3, Ross composes a memorable epistolary exchange between Helen and Christine/Oreo (pp. 23–24):

> When Christine was three and Jimmie C. two, Helen's letters read:
>
> > Pittsburgh [or wherever]
> Mommy would give anything to just stay at home and take care of her precious babies.
>
> Christine stared at the letter for some time, then, carefully selecting her Crayolas (a huge set that boasted exotic colors like red, green, and blue as well as the standard mauve, puce, chartreuse, and oregano), she composed a reply:
>
> > Philadelphia
> dear mom cut the crap

I do not think that it is an interpretation too far to suggest that the three-year-old Christine is able to see through her mother's excuses because she knows the classical commonplace that her mother is exploiting—namely Helen's expression of regret about eloping with Paris to Troy, abandoning her marriage, her male relatives, and her child in Book 3 of Homer's *Iliad*:

> If only death had pleased me then, grim death,
> The day I followed your son to Troy, forsaking
> My marriage bed, my kinsmen and my child,
> My favourite, my fully-grown.
> *(Iliad* 3.173–175, trans. Fagles)

As a precocious wunderkind, Christine/Oreo also knows the fragment of Sappho that writes back to Homer's depiction of Helen. Like Helen of Troy, as reimagined in fragment 16 of Sappho, Christine's mother 'never spent a thought on her child or loving parents.'[49] Re-versioning does not get more sassy than the young Christine's mirror-writing to turn a classical trope back on her mother with help from Sappho and a healthy dose of the vernacular muse ('cut the crap'). This is Sappho taken off her pedestal as the tenth muse.

In her foreword to the 2000 edition of Fran Ross' *Oreo*, Mullen introduces an idiosyncratic ('more eccentric than Afrocentric') author who exemplifies many traits that readers associate with Mullen's poetry, not least *Muse & Drudge*: '*Oreo* is a text that assumes the verbal intelligence, the linguistic and cultural competence of readers who appreciate the rich diversity that contributes to the complexity of their own identities' (Mullen in Ross, *Oreo*, xxviii). There are benefits to being a-mused: the right to complexity is one of them.

Notes

1. Mullen, *Recyclopedia*, xi.
2. In a recent volume, Michele Kennerly has put forward a new manifesto of classical rhetorical theory in which the alpha privative is used to invert and complicate the familiar classical terms. See Kennerly, *A New Handbook*, 12–13. I use the passive participle *a*mused in honor of Mullen's untiring word

plays and in reference to Kennerly's work on the rhetorical use of the alpha privative.

3. Mackey, 'Other,' 68, and 52.
4. Mullen, 'Imagining,' 199.
5. Henderson, 'Speaking,' 17, drawing on Smith's idea of the 'simultaneity of discourse' in black women's writing (Smith, *Home Girls*, xxxii), and 22.
6. The phrase 'creative dialogue' is also from Smith, quoted in Henderson, 'Speaking,' 19.
7. Ahmed, *What's the Use?*
8. Mullen, *Recylcopedia*, 99. On further creative misuse in this opening line, see p. 424–427 below.
9. Fuss, *Essentially Speaking*, 83.
10. Mullen, *The Cracks Between*, 19.
11. Lorde, *Selected Works*, 82.
12. The Combahee River Collective reprinted in Taylor, *How We Get Free*, 18–19.
13. Mullen examined this spectrum in an interview with Calvin Bedient, recorded in 1996 (Mullen, *The Cracks Between*, 194–195): 'There's a range of representations from the diva to the debased woman—the muse, the drudge. Those are the polarities. Those are the extreme oppositions that we see in representations of black women in the media. Either the fabulous diva or the mother using crack, the prostitute. The super-skinny black model versus Aunt Jemima. I was interested in more of a continuum, filling in or troubling those kinds of oppositional constructions of black women.'
14. Hamer in Brooks and Houck, *Speeches*, 97–103, quoting from p. 98.
15. Hurston, *Their Eyes Were Watching God: A Novel*, 16.
16. See Mullen, *The Cracks Between*, 200–201 for discussion, and 19 for the word play 'mules and drugs.' For the trope of the black woman as mule, see Collins, *Black Feminist Thought*, 14, and 51.
17. Using undercommons after Moten and Harney, *The Undercommons*. See Mix, 'Inspiration,' 57 on the gendered constraints on the muse in classical epic.
18. Bennett, *Being Property*, 114–139, quoting from p. 117. For the linking of 'mule' and 'drudge' in a recent work exploring narrativity as both a scene of constraint and a site of radical possibility, see Hartman's stream of consciousness narration

for Eva and Aaron, 'What kind of woman could be treated as a mule or drudge, reduced to hands and ass, worked like a man and treated like a slave?' (Hartman, *Wayward Lives*, 274).

19. In an interview with Elisabeth Frost in 2000, reprinted in Mullen, *The Cracks Between*, 213–232, Mullen mentioned that she used the translation of Callimachus' *Aetia* by Diane Rayor (and Stanley Lombardo), in the anthology *Latin Lyric and Elegiac Poetry*. The *Aetia* translation appears as an appendix to this volume: Rayor and Batstone, *Latin Lyric*, 339–342.

20. Shockley, *Renegade Poetics*, 82.

21. Mullen, *The Cracks Between*, 262.

22. Mullen, *Recyclopedia*, xi. Mullen and Rayor were contemporaries in graduate school at the University of California at Santa Cruz. Writing of her approach to translating Sappho, Rayor writes, 'Through specific choice of words and style, the translations here reflect my individual response to the ancient poetry. My response is informed by knowledge of Greek and of the historical context of the poetry. My gender, my background in contemporary American culture, and my personal enjoyment of contemporary American poetry also influence that response' (Rayor, *Sappho's Lyre*, 18, 'Translator's Note').

23. In the interview with Elizabeth Frost (see n.19 above), Mullen mentioned that Rayor had claimed that Mullen had used her translation of Sappho 'without citation,' and points out that, in punning on the title of Rayor 1991 in the first line of *Muse & Drudge* she had made the debt explicit (Mullen, *The Cracks Between*, 220).

24. Mullen, *Recyclopedia*, vii. All three collections recycle multiple works in different media, but the major literary sources being adapted in the first two collections are Gertrude Stein's novel *Tender Buttons* (1914), while Sappho's fragmentary corpus is the major adapted corpus in *Muse & Drudge*.

25. See Mansell, 'Hearing,' 131–133, quoting from p. 133.

26. On 'bi-translation', see Fuss cited on p. 421 above.

27. Frost, 'Ruses,' 469–472; Spahr, *Everybody's Autonomy*, 111–114; Frost, *The Feminist Avant-Garde*, 157–159; Hart, *Nations of Nothing*, 150–153; Mix, 'Inspiration,' 55; and Scroggins, *Intricate Thicket*, 202–203.

28. Perloff, 'After Language Poetry,' 30.

29. Hart, *Nations of Nothing*, 155.

30. Reed, *Freedom Time*, 136. Shockley, *Renegade Poetics*, 82–112

offers an original reading of *Muse & Drudge* as a blues epic
with the blues as formal inspiration, source, and medium for
poetic innovation.

31. Spahr, *Everybody's Autonomy*, 112. Frost, 'Ruses,' 471 was
    the first scholar to make this connection in print.
32. See Davis, *Blues Legacies*, 338 for the lyrics.
33. See Winkler, 'Gardens of Nymphs,' 104: '*Mēlon*, convention-
    ally translated "apple," is really a general word for fleshy fruit
    – apricots, peaches, apples, citron, quinces, pomegranates.'
34. See Frost, *The Feminist Avant-Garde*, 158–159. The line
    'whose lives are lovely too,' puns on the final lyric of Billy
    Strayhorn's song 'Lush Life' (initially composed in 1933
    and recorded in 1948): 'whose lives are lonely, too' (I thank
    Christopher Waldo for drawing this to my attention). Frost,
    'Ruses,' 470 notes that the phrases 'plucked eyebrows' and
    'bow lips and legs' also reference the double bass, plucked and
    played with the bow.
35. Mansell, 'Hearing,' 127. Mansell offers a thorough analysis
    of Mullen's modulation of different genres of black music. For
    Jazz specifically, see Ryan, *Post-Jazz Poetics*.
36. Scroggins, *Intricate Thicket*, 203; see also Perloff, 'After
    Language Poetry,' 30.
37. Mullen explained the context for the photograph, taken by a
    friend of her publisher Gil Ott, in an interview with Elisabeth
    Frost: 'It is an ambiguous image which I liked' (Mullen, *The
    Cracks Between*, 224).
38. Griffin, 'When Malindy Sings,' 104.
39. Mullen, *Recylcopedia*, 115.
40. Horace, *Ars Poetica*, 128–131.
41. Ellison, 'The Little Man,' 30–31. Initially delivered as a lecture
    in Philadelphia on May 10, 1975 with the title 'The Little Man
    Behind the Stove.'
42. On Mullen's 'synthetic vernacular poetry,' see Hart, *Nations of
    Nothing*, 149–156.
43. For discussion of how the discourse of adaptation and rever-
    sioning in this quatrain echoes throughout *Muse & Drudge*,
    see Mix, 'Inspiration,' 65.
44. Sharpe, *In the Wake*, 96 defines the 'dysgraphia' of the wake
    as, 'the inability of language to cohere around the bodies and
    the suffering of those Black people who live and die in the wake
    and whose everyday acts insist Black life into the wake.'

45. See Philip, *She Tries Her Tongue*, 81 on the English language as 'etymologically hostile and expressive of the non-being of the African.'
46. Gubar, 'Sapphistries,' 202.
47. See Spahr, *Everybody's Autonomy*, 114, who notes the resonance of 'Sappho's role as one of the first "outsider" poets' for Mullen's adaptation of Sappho at the beginning of *Muse & Drudge*. In the first black womanist manifesto, Anna Julia Cooper's *A Voice from the South*, Cooper cites Sappho as an enabling precedent (Cooper, *A Voice*, 68–69). In the same period, Pauline Hopkins named one of the protagonists of her novel *Contending Forces* (1900) Sappho Clark (a pseudonym in the novel) and made her a book-loving stenographer, like Hopkins herself.
48. The mythological key spans pp. 209–212 of Ross, *Oreo*.
49. Sappho fr.16, lines 10–11, in Diane Rayor's translation, 'She had no | memory of her child or dear parents, | since she was led astray' (Rayor, *Sappho's Lyre*, 55).

A Poetics of Interrogation: Collective Readership and Authorial Plenum in *Muse & Drudge*

Solveig Daugaard

The mythology of the independent, self-sufficient author and the apparition of the silent, solitary reader receiving and mirroring this author's inner vision in secluded interiority are both foundational elements in the technological construction of the modern bourgeois individual that binds this figure to the medium of print literature. Cybernetic thinker and literary critic N. Katherine Hayles has suggested thinking of the current media situation of literature in terms of 'postprint.' Not to postulate that print has ended, but rather to recognise the massive changes in 'how books are composed, edited, designed, warehoused, distributed, inventoried, sold, and read' that the gradual introduction of computational technology into the print industry has imposed.[1] According to Hayles, a distribution of agency in all phases of book production has taken place, and her analysis suggests a loosening of the ties between print books and the self-sufficient individual of modernity and feeds into the discussions of the 'posthuman' that she has been leading in her work over the past decades.

However, as book historian Leah Price points out, much recent discourse on print literature tends to stick to a dichotomy of competition when faced with the rise of digital media. Consequently, the reading of books is treated, not only as a silent and isolated pastime in contrast to other artistic media received in crowds at museums, public spaces, concert halls, and theatres but as a veritable 'training for solitary self-sufficiency' that we are at risk of losing access to due to the constant distractions of our digital devices. The challenge to print from digital media over the past decades has, according to Price, evoked a widespread nostalgia, idealising the production of 'a certain kind of individual' through the solitary, immersive reading of print.[2] The changed conditions of print literature have not only led to idealisation of the (threatened) individuality of the reader, but they also produce and prominently feature the countenance of the sovereign, accountable author. In the complex media ecology in which print is currently immersed, the author's body, face, voice, and biographical yarns are drawn into the circulation of a written work, turning the author's persona into an affective interface distributed across platforms through which literature is accessed by its readers, whether they are conscious of it or not. Further, this mechanism interpellates the author to inhabit the individualised interface of an exclusive art system and nudges him or her to perform as the self-sufficient and fully responsible source of the work.[3] If, in the media history of western modernity, alphabetic writing has been cast as the media technological mold of the modern individual, then even as we enter a postprint era this connection stubbornly dominates the ways in which we conceptualise literature. In short, literature still produces separate, enclosed individuals: writers as well as readers.

One way to challenge this agenda could be to shift our perspective and, as Price encourages us, to consider books less as a technology of self-sufficiency and more as 'a means to connect the human beings who exchange them'.[4] Such a shift can be observed in the turn to coproduction and community formation in recent scholarship in book history, focusing, for instance, on historical and contemporary small press publishing.[5] The reception of Harryette Mullen's fourth collection of poetry, *Muse & Drudge* (1995) offers another way to approach such a shift, rich as it is with accounts of the delights produced by this eighty-page-long poem when removed from the enclosure of solitary reading and read in a plenum.[6] Although the college classroom is hardly an unusual place to engage with innovative poetry (on the contrary, in empirical reality it is probably the single situation where most readers are first confronted with such writing), it is, in accordance with Price's point, surprisingly rare for scholarship on experimental poetry – unless explicitly pedagogic in its focus – to front collective reading situations. Rather, as academic readers of poetry, we tend to construct our 'auto-bibliographies' as individual achievements, cut loose from the formative support of professors, librarians, pedagogues, and parents. But the way Mullen's polyvocal serial poem interweaves multifarious scraps of language from sources ranging not just across most linguistic genres imaginable but also over 2,000 years and several continents, creates a complex texture of poetic language within the deceivingly simple form of the quatrain, which is endlessly generative when read in a group. The poem employs so many different registers in every line that no single reader is likely to master them, making the immediate benefit of breaking the silence and solitude of conventional readership unmistakable. Thus, the reading patterns Mullen's poems encourage are far from the idealised immersive, consecutive long-reads sustaining carceral individuals. Rather, they suggest distracted, interrogational jump cuts, that connect different readers, and force them to exchange.

In discussing *Muse & Drudge*, Mullen herself confirms her intention to create an inclusive readership that transgressed racial, cultural, and social divides. Yet, in the light of the successful collective reading experiences her poems have indeed generated, it is striking how immediately conflictual her motivation for wanting to transcend the position of the solitary reader, is. It derives from an essentially uncomfortable situation, regarding her performance as an embodied author vis-à-vis a live audience. In essays and interviews given in the years surrounding the publication, she returns to the experience of giving public readings from her two preceding collections, *Trimmings* (1991) and *S*PeRM**K*T* (1992) in which she had reworked Gertrude Stein's avant-garde classic *Tender Buttons* (1914), and suddenly found herself to be the only person of colour in the room, in stark contrast to her experience when reading from her earlier work in which she had worked with a more unified, vernacular poetic voice.[7] It added to the uneasiness when readers suggested to her, that with *Trimmings* she had begun writing less 'black' than in her previous poetry because the writing was more 'experimental'. Mullen's enhanced experience of authorial confinement makes explicit the casualties that the individualised, self-sufficient, and – in the increasingly immersive media environment of the 1990s – highly exposed authorial position implies for poets of colour in a literary public tainted by what she coined as an 'aesthetic apartheid'[8] in reference to the implied, but cleverly concealed, whiteness of the categories of 'avant-garde', 'innovative', or 'experimental' poetry. Mullen's ingenious analysis of the aesthetic apartheid surrounding American avant-garde poetry, which has become further established in subsequent scholarship on the poetics of the post-war avant-garde[9] and the black radical tradition,[10] departs from the immediate unavailability of the position of experimental writer to her as a black woman (also) wanting black readership in a literary public sphere where minority writers were cast, anthologised, and circulated as primarily experiential rather than experimental and expected to express a solid group identity rather than to destabilise constraining logics of representation and identity on a fundamental level. The striking paradox regarding the institutional recognition of formal innovation in African American poetry that Mullen points to is outlined by poetry historian Lauri Ramey, namely 'that truly original poetry, ironically, has been considered the domain of the poets with the greatest access to centers of cultural power which they have the authority to challenge and disrupt with eventual acceptance.'[11]

At stake in the highly marked position of Mullen as a black woman entertaining a room (or, by extension, a reading public) of, however sympathetically predisposed, white people, is firstly, the intersectional rancor that historically sticks to the position of the African American woman poet, and secondly, the racialising mechanisms at work in the transitional media culture of the 1990s. The first factor can be framed by the trial against the first published black poet in America, Phillis Wheatley (1753–1784), labeled by Henry Louis Gates, Jr. as 'the primal scene of African-American letters'.[12] The 19-year-old enslaved Wheatley was not only forced to stand before a panel of white, slave-owning 'men of letters' not convinced that the 'African race' was capable of such a degree of literacy, to authenticate that her poetry was indeed written by her, but has also, posthumously, been subjected to repeated accusations of 'race betrayal'. In the words of Black Arts critic Addison Gayle, Jr., for instance, Wheatley was guilty of 'accept[ing] the images and symbols of degradation' of Southern racist discourse and hereby 'surrender[ing] the right to self-definition to others'.[13] Writing in the poetic tradition available to her, that of her enslavers, and being called to certify the authenticity of her writing with her black body, Wheatley's example incarnates the exposure, vulnerability, and potential violence, both physical and discursive, that historically sticks to the position of the American black female poet. And the harshness with which she has been treated by posterity, as exemplified by (primarily male) critics of the Black Arts tradition, stresses how its call to black separatism did not immediately have the same supportive impact upon this position as it had on the position of the black poet who was also male and heterosexual.

The second factor involves the interpellation of the author to perform as an individualised incarnation of her work. Although hardly as elaborate then as we experience it today where social media profiles are integrated parts of most writers' channel to the public, a potential commodification of the racialised persona is at play in Mullen's example. This recalls intersectional feminist bell hooks' concept of 'eating the Other' as established through her analysis of the 'consumer cannibalism' of white hegemonic culture toward the racialised Other in American popular culture of the early 1990s.[14] Here, according to hooks, a fundamentally racist desire toward racial difference is both thriving and increasingly concealed as it becomes dressed up as multiculturalist inclusiveness. In hooks' account, this cultural mechanism becomes a strong argument for black nationalism as 'a survival strategy' for 'black people [. . .] to protect themselves from this kind of objectifying interaction'.[15] hooks' vision of separatism is informed by black feminism and comes from a recognition of individual differences among black women united by 'the desire to create a context where one can "love blackness" as a worthy standpoint for bonding, even if such bonding must take the form of self-segregation'.[16]

Yet, confronted with the uncomfortable racialising isolation of her author's persona, Mullen with *Muse & Drudge* appears to move toward creating a dialogic, even a conflictual, space for exchange across differences, rather than a safe space of self-segregation. As she phrases it: 'There is [. . .] a social discomfort, a personal discomfort [. . .] when I find that my language is not understood or that I don't understand someone else's language [. . .]'.[17] With discomfort and awkwardness as its point of departure, Mullen's poetic strategy still insists on its dialogic mode. Instead of directly negating, countering, or denying the structures of racialisation traversing the world of avant-garde poetry, and withdrawing from this discriminatory poetry world to establish an alternative separatist community free of such structures, her innovative poetic strategy is one of 'interrogation' that involves keeping many positions open but not unchallenged. As she stresses: 'innovation is interrogative' in the sense of 'standing between and asking questions'.[18] Pondering 'what in [her] work was keeping people of color out of the room',[19] the idea came to her of merging the figures of Sappho, the mother of the lyric poetry fragment, with Sapphire, the racial stereotype of the 'angry black woman', and blues singers such as Ma Rainey and Bessie Smith, adding scraps of modernist poetry, fragments from the Black Arts tradition, news media discourse, commercial culture and vernacular, folk cultural forms of black (and white) America. In the poem, an emphatic poetic voice is created that claims itself distinctly like that of a blues singer yet also remains playfully patched together from a chorus of voices. Sometimes mutually contradictory and interrogating each other, or, in the manner of the Sapphire-figure, 'talking back', they serve as an incarnation of the 'consent not to be a single being' that poet and thinker Fred Moten has promoted as a headline for Black Studies. Like Moten's use of the motto, lifted from an interview with Martinican philosopher Édouard Glissant,[20] the poem insists on the ability to both realise and persistently reject the racial segregation and violent discourse of anti-blackness facing black life and in the same breath celebrate the autonomy, richness, and plurality of such life, all through phrases borrowed, recycled, and twisted. Surely, in the establishment of this plenum of voices, lies part of the key to Mullen's success with uniting, in *Muse & Drudge*, the separate readerships of her earlier poetry. This new union, however, is very different from the commodification of difference negating the history of the Other, as analysed by hooks. Both because it, in accordance with Moten's line, starts from the black experience, and not the white gaze upon it, and because it embraces the conflictual element in such difference, or it adopts a practice of 'interrogation' toward the discomforts it carries along, rather than attempting to iron them out.

Yet however plural the poetic voice(s) arising from its pages, the isolation of the authorial agent standing behind the collection is still complying with the technological and juridical framework of print literature. Mullen, by writing another book of poetry with her name on the cover, is obviously also committed to the institutionalised infrastructures of poetic production that enforce individual authorship through copyright. But as I will now discuss, her collection challenges this on multiple levels, from the curation of intertextual sources, over the manipulation of linguistic microlayers, to the infrastructural attachments and functionalities involving the material base, paratextual framing, and readerly circulation of her poetry.

The literary sources that *Muse & Drudge* draws on are multiple. Many come with nametags such as puns on specific titles including 'up from slobbery' punning on Booker T. Washington's autobiography and 'the soles of black feet'[21] on W.E.B. Du Bois' 1903 classic book title, or characteristic quotes such as the 'wide abandoned laughter',[22] recalling the recurring racist predicate that is used to describe the simple, sorrowless mentality of black people in Gertrude Stein's story 'Melanctha': 'the wide abandoned laughter that gives the broad glow to negro sunshine'.[23] But they are supplemented by multiple references to folk-art forms that involve distributed authorship and oral archiving. Forms from what performance scholar Diana Taylor would label 'the repertoire' – including the oral performance in contrast to the written archive[24] – are reappearing throughout the poem which also includes quotes from plantation songs (i.e. 'old time religion', 'under the drinking gourd'), figures and puns picked from streetwise oral forms such as the dozens as well as quilting, assemblage, and contemporary community art projects like the Heidelberg houses in Detroit.[25] All artworks and practices that deliberately challenge the elitist system of art based on individual authorship. As Ramey has stressed, the question of authorship is a highly problematic one when discussing the cultural products of 'an enslaved and oppressed population that was legally deprived of literacy'.[26] In extension, naively romanticising the anonymous or collective authorship of indigenous and black culture would be wrong, but it remains crucial that Mullen's poem, alongside its many references to named and authored works of art and literature, features a set of artistic traditions not in their first instance controlled by the production of individual authorship, and not initially interfaced through it.

As Evie Shockley points out, readings of the collection as a 'culturally hybrid' work run a poignant risk of 'unintentionally reinforc[ing] certain white/black binaries that privilege "whiteness" as the source of order, theory, and concept and relegate "blackness" to the realm of raw product, the "stuff" which can be abstracted into an intellectually grounded art via the right experimental approaches'.[27] This risk would also apply if one were to establish a stable opposition between the 'black' collective art practices of the 'repertoire' and the 'white' print culture 'archive' of juridical copyright and individual authorship, including the literary tradition produced by European descendants (from Sappho over Shakespeare and Isaac Watts to Gertrude Stein) and the 'sharp white background' of the commercial publishing industry appropriating and packaging black poetry (i.e. 'white covers of black material'[28]). Mullen has addressed the opposition between orality and literacy in a critique of the tendency to equate blackness with oral culture, and reached for a more feminist approach to writing as a challenge to the patriarchal model of authorship and control. The latter she illustrates with Frederick Douglass' autobiography where he stresses the determination and masculine self-sufficiency it took to acquire the prohibited skill of writing, and how he used it to construct himself as a free individual, while Harriet Jacobs among others provides an alternative feminist and collaborative model of reading and writing acquired and practiced in a community of women.[29]

The complications can be projected through the ambiguous figure behind the collection's epigraph, the ancient poet Callimachus (c. 310–240 BC), most prominently remembered as a librarian at the Library of Alexandria, and author of the world's first library catalogue, the *Pinakes*. This work was the backbone of antiquity's most significant institution for preserving and exchanging written knowledge. Here, Callimachus listed the Greek language works of the library, and his bibliography was organised through an alphabetically sorted author-title system like we use today. In this sense, through the cultural technique of cataloguing, the *Pinakes* produced individually responsible authors while at the same time supplying the very infrastructure that provides the 'recyclopedias' Mullen's work draws upon[30] and in practice turns books into 'a means to connect the human beings who exchange them'. In this sense, a double logic of separability and community is inscribed into the ancient history of the written word. Furthermore, the fact that the Library of Alexandria was located on the African continent, and the biography of Callimachus, who – although most surviving 'portraits' of him today are in shining white marble – as a Greek born in Libya was most likely 'brown as toast Egyptian'.[31] elegantly complicates the artificial segregation of European and African cultural history by suggesting the extensive African investments in the origins of writing, libraries, and literature constructed as purely European by the 'history written with whitening'[32] called out by *Muse & Drudge*.

Despite the chorus of voices – named and unnamed, individual, and generic – speaking in *Muse & Drudge*, the authorial attribution of the text remains undeniably Harryette Mullen's. But even on the level of authorial signature, Mullen is challenging the carceral model of the individual through her interrogational poetic strategy. In several passages the poem works with deliberate opacity as lines and entire stanzas approach rhythmic nonsense verse associated with scat singing. As Brent Hayes Edwards points out, the practice of scatting is a way of radically dissolving the individuality of words and, by extension, the transparency of the speaker as a coherent person communicating a message to a listener.[33] One of the poem's most scat-like quatrains reads as sonically carefully patterned but semantically approaching the nonsensical. It opens with the stanza:

> marry at a hotel, annul 'em
> nary hep male rose sullen
> let alley roam, yell melon
> dull normal fellow hammers omelette[34]

Behind its immediate semantic oddness, this stanza plays with the letters of the poet's name 'Harryette Romell Mullen', which are repeated and cast around in new constellations all through the stanza, thus creating a concealed authorial signature within the poem, in the manner of Shakespeare in his sonnets.[35] These concealed epithets have been somewhat contested in scholarship on Shakespeare, due to the obvious difficulty of proving that a centuries-deceased author deliberately placed a well-hidden code in his text, and the tendency to find whatever one is looking for when approaching poetry as a coded word puzzle. In this quatrain, the succeeding stanzas resemble the first in containing a limited number of letters and phonemes repeated through four semantically enigmatic but sonically tightly woven lines, suggesting that other names might be hidden in them, although which ones does not immediately reveal itself.

Perchance like a lot of the readers in the all-white audience Mullen encountered when reading from *Trimmings* and *S*PeRM**K*T*, I first came to her poetry through avant-garde and modernism studies by way of Gertrude Stein, whose poetic reception Mullen's work has comprehensively reshaped.[36] And with my baggage in Stein scholarship, I too have a way of finding what I am looking for. Going out from the immediately opaque second line of the stanza 'nary hep male rose sullen', I could not help but see a reference to the perhaps single most problematic racial stereotype in Stein's oeuvre, the character Rose Johnson from the story 'Melanctha' already evoked in an earlier quatrain. Rose Johnson is the friend of the story's title character, and in the story, the personalities of the two women are repeatedly tied to their skin tones (which are ironically swapped in relation to the colors suggested by their first names – Melanctha being derived from the Greek root 'melan' meaning black) with the 'pale mulatto Melanctha' depicted as intelligent, complex, and restless while the 'dark-skinned negro' Rose is described as stupid, self-absorbed, and, most frequently, 'sullen'. In extension, the marriage and its annulment of the first line speaks to legal regulations of individuals, and recalls how, in Stein's story, Rose is very preoccupied with being respectably married, yet is too careless to prevent her own baby from dying when left alone with it for a few days. The also rather cryptic subsequent line 'let alley roam, yell melon' resonates with the name and complexion of the story's title character, who is described as yellow-skinned and 'wandering'.

Several studies that have traced Mullen's treatment of Stein's work conclude that Mullen, with her rewriting of *Tender Buttons*, is 'trimming the racism out of Stein'.[37] Yet, in this quatrain something quite different is going on. Mullen is indeed interrogating the racism in Stein's story, but not in the manner of denying or eliminating it. By constructing an authorial signature poem like Shakespeare's out of the Rose Johnson figure, Mullen inhabits the racism of Stein, who famously made her own signature out of the figure of the rose, and unmasks the implicit whiteness dressed up as universality in poetic modernism, while interweaving it with her own authorial signature. The practice of scatting relates to the way Stein in her writing turns language into physical material rather than transparent communication by tearing it up and piecing it together in new ways. Or, as Edwards points out in his discussion of scat, by literally 'talking shit', both in the sense of speaking incorrectly, talking rough or dirty, and in the sense of applying scatological imagery while insisting on a right to opacity.[38] If Phillis Wheatley was once harshly accused of letting others define her as a black American, Mullen demonstrates that committing to black separatism does not dispose of the white gaze once and for all. By letting her own signature get mixed up with the white tradition of English poetry, Shakespeare's anagrammatic tricks, and Stein's racial stereotype, she refrains from a separatist stance.

A drama of problematic racialisation from "Melanctha" is played out but at the same time the stanza remains an instance of improvisational, obscure, self-effacing scat-poetry, and carefully coded namesake. Tying together these three elements in one stanza: the literary tradition of English language modernism in an anti-black instantiation, the improvisatory black song tradition of scat, and her own author's signature, enigmatically tucked under the racial drama and the nonsense-verse, and presented as potentially arbitrary, as one among the many voices that are heard in this poem, makes a strong point.

Rather than erasing racist figures that permeate literary culture, the collection follows the advice of its epigraph and 'fattens [its] animal for sacrifice' – inhabiting, owning, and blowing up the racial stereotypes and tying them to the individual author's signature that is, in turn, partially dissolved into a tapestry of collective authorship. As *Muse & Drudge* stubbornly stays with its own trouble, its author is also fighting isolation by collectivising authorship, in the poems and sources she draws on, and in the design of the book itself.

As a means of reaching the intended readership which she felt she had lost with her previous two books, Mullen addresses the question of pre-reading. In the 1990s, book design was not as common a concern as it has become with the 'aesthetics of bookishness' that has come to flourish in the postprint era. Yet, Mullen had reasons for earnestly involving herself in the book's material design, as she has explained:

> Usually, the covers of books don't say, Here is a black poet, but I have become very aware of the protocols, the blurbs and what's on the cover. You can tell a black book fifteen feet away, by the cover. The color is usually much brighter than other books, with maybe a kente pattern in the design. Usually there is a black icon or a black person. There are signals that say this is yours or it is not yours.[39]

The visual signs of the black book that Mullen refers to were largely developed in the independent publishing wave of the Black Arts Movement, with its strong will to prevent 'white covers of black materials' and keep white publishers from capitalising on the cultural revolution produced by black artists by obtaining black control over the means of poetic production. Most obviously, the colors black and blue that dominate the cover and the photograph on the front speak to this tradition, yet Mullen's book is also clearly hacking it. In some critical notes on the collection from the time of its publication, its cover photo is mistaken for a portrait of the book's author. And it very well could have been, if following the design traditions of Broadside or Third World Press, which often put large authors' portraits on their covers, signaling the racial attributes of the author as a crucial characteristic of a book that needed to be communicated first-hand to its readers. Instead, Mullen modified the cover photo by xerox-copying it, and ended up with an almost anonymised, yet affectively intense, soulful image of a 'generic' black woman, to match the poem's generic voice of the blues singer, and omitted the otherwise obligatory author's portrait and bio, thus on yet another level interweaving her author's identity with a group of others. The colophon, organised by the Callimachean author-title principle but also explicitly hacking it, is another paratext that echoes this gesture. The spot securing a book's juridical copyright to its author, Mullen's unusual inclusion inside its frame of an elaborate section acknowledging the collaborate circumstances around the book's production, including the shared authorship of the book's graphic design and the contributions of Singing Horse publisher Gil Ott, numerous journal editors as well as an artistic collaboration setting the poem to music, urges us to read poetic authorship as a fundamentally collaborative endeavor. As she writes in the dedication in another of her books: 'This book is dedicated to family and friends. Without them I could never have written anything at all'.[40] Outside the immediate banality of such a declaration of gratitude toward the people with whom the author shares her life, this statement points to a collaborative aspect in all poetic writing, that people writing have rarely had an interest in recognising, just like literary scholars have not had an interest in recognising the collaborative nature of reading. In the 1990s, black feminist poetry was submitted to an intersectionally enhanced infrastructural pressure, forcing it to consider questions of pre-reading, paratext, and circulation and to fight the isolation of the confessional authorial self-exposure, that, as bell hooks describes, offers itself to hegemonic culture's cannibalistic desire of 'eating the Other'. 'I don't think there's an automatic linkage between being marginalised or oppressed and being innovative', Mullen assures 'but I do think that being oppressed does call upon all of your resources, and often out of that comes innovation'.[41] The understanding of writing and reading as collaborative and entangled activities runs through the voices, the motives, the book design, and the paratexts of *Muse & Drudge*. In this way, Mullen creates a strong community of solidarity and shared authorship around her book inseparable from the communitarian effects of its inclusive reception, and effectively challenging the fetishisation of individual authorship: We always write in collaboration with the readers we can imagine.

Notes

1. N. Katherine Hayles, *Postprint. Books and Becoming Computational* (New York: Columbia University Press, 2021), 2.
2. Leah Price, *What we Talk About When we Talk About Books: The History and Future of Reading* (New York: Basic Books, 2018), 9.
3. See also Solveig Daugaard, *Collaborating with Gertrude Stein. Media Ecologies, Reception, Poetics* (PhD diss., Linköping University, 2018) and Daugaard et al. "Preface Collective," *Peripeti*, Vol. 31 (March, 2020), 21–36.
4. Price, *What we Talk About*, 9.
5. For example Colby et al., *The Contemporary Small Press: Making Publishing Visible* (Cham: Palgrave Macmillan, 2020).
6. For summary of this vein in its reception, see e.g. Allison Cummings, "Public Subjects: Race and the Critical Reception of Gwendolyn Brooks, Erica Hunt, and Harryette Mullen," *Frontiers: A Journal of Women Studies*, Vol. 26, No. 2 (2005), 3–36.
7. See e.g., "Poetry and Identity," "Imagining the Unimagined Reader," "Kinky Quatrains," and interviews included in Mullen, *The Cracks Between What We Are and What We Are Supposed to Be* (Tuscaloosa: The University of Alabama Press, 2012) and the untitled essay by Mullen in *Tripwire: a journal of poetics*, No. 5 (Fall 2001), 11–14.
8. "Poetry and Identity," 12.
9. For example Timothy Yu, *Race and the Avant-Garde: Experimental and Asian American Poetry Since 1965* (Stanford, CA: Stanford University Press, 2009), and Cathy Park Hong, "Delusions of Whiteness in the Avant-Garde," *Lana Turner*, Vol. 7 (2015).
10. For example Fred Moten, *In the Break. The Aesthetics of the Black Radical Tradition* (London: University of Minnesota Press, 2003), Anthony Reed, *Freedom Time. The Poetics*

and Politics of Black Experimental Writing (Baltimore, MD: Johns Hopkins University Press, 2014), and Denise Ferreira da Silva, "Toward a Black Feminist Poethics. The Quest(ion) of Blackness Toward the End of the World," *The Black Scholar: Journal of Black Studies and Research*, Vol. 44, No. 2 (2014).

11. Lauri Ramey, *A History of African American Poetry* (Cambridge: Cambridge University Press, 2019), 10–11.
12. Henry Louis Gates, Jr., "A Critic at Large: Phillis Wheatley on Trial," *New Yorker*, January 12, 2003, 82.
13. Quoted in Gates, "A Critic at Large," 87.
14. bell hooks, *Black Looks: Race and Representation* (Boston, MA: South End Press, 1992).
15. Ibid., 17.
16. Ibid.
17. Harryette Mullen, untitled essay, *Tripwire*, 13.
18. Ibid., 12.
19. Ibid., 13.
20. Moten uses the line as overarching headline of his trilogy consisting of *Black and Blur* (Durham, NC: Duke University Press, 2017), *Stolen Life* (Durham, NC: Duke University Press, 2018), and *The Universal Machine* (Durham, NC: Duke University Press, 2018).
21. Both, Harryette Mullen, *Muse & Drudge* (Philadelphia, PA: Singing Horse Press, 1995), 46.
22. Ibid., 54.
23. Gertrude Stein, *Writings 1903–1932* (New York: Library of America 1998), e.g. 124, 219.
24. Diana Taylor, *The Archive and The Repertoire. Performing Cultural Memory in the Americas* (Durham, NC: Duke University Press, 2003).
25. See Mullen, *Muse & Drudge*, 14, 26, 70, 32, 76.
26. Ramey, *A History of African American Poetry*, 15.
27. Evie Shockley, *Renegade Poetics. Black Aesthetics and Formal Innovation in African American Poetry* (Iowa City: Iowa University Press, 2011), 84–85.
28. Mullen, *Muse & Drudge*, 32.
29. Haryette Mullen, "Runaway Tongue: Resistant Orality in *Uncle Tom's Cabin, Our Nig, Incidents in the Life of a Slave Girl*, and *Beloved*," in *The Cracks Between*, 102–129.
30. See Mullen, *Muse & Drudge*, 68 and "Recycle this Book," in Harryette Mullen, *Recyclopedia: Trimmings, S*PeRM**K*T,*

and *Muse & Drudge* (Saint Paul, MN: Graywolf Press 2006), vii.

31. Mullen, *Muse & Drudge*, 45.
32. Ibid.
33. Brent Hayes Edwards, *Epistrophies. Jazz and the Literary Imagination* (Cambridge, MA: Harvard University Press, 2017), 27–56.
34. Mullen, *Muse & Drudge*, 64.
35. See for instance, R.H. Winnick, "'Loe, here in one line is his name twice writ': Anagrams, Shakespeare's Sonnets, and the Identity of the Fair Friend," in *Literary Imagination*, Vol. 11, No. 3, 2009.
36. See Daugaard "'I'm always wanting to collaborate with some one': The Performative Poetics of Gertrude Stein and its Reception as Collaboration," in Hættner Aurelius et al. (ed.), *Performativity in Literature. The Lund–Nanjing Seminars*, Konferenser 91 (Stockholm: Kungliga Vitterhetsakademien, 2016), 232–246.
37. Deborah Mix, *A Vocabulary of Thinking. Gertrude Stein and Contemporary North American Women's Innovative Writing* (Iowa City: University of Iowa Press, 2007), 46.
38. Edwards, *Epistrophies*, 27–56.
39. "An Interview with Harryette Mullen by Elizabeth A. Frost," in Mullen, *The Cracks Between*, 229.
40. Mullen, *The Cracks Between*, vi.
41. Mullen, untitled essay, *Tripwire*, 12.

Recycling Shakespeare: Mullen and the Lyric Tradition

Ayesha Ramachandran

A favorite, seemingly inevitable question confronts Harryette Mullen in almost every published interview. "I wanted to ask you about the question of audience in your work," remarks Elizabeth Frost (1997); "How do you position your work?" asks Cynthia Hogue (1999); "I'm interested in your attention to audience," prods Daniel Kane (2003); "While composing a poem, do you have a particular audience in mind?" probes Nibir Ghosh (2005); "Has the audience(s) you are addressing and the manner of that address changed in each of your books?" asks Caroline Crumpacker (2014).[1] Few contemporary poets have been so plagued by the dilemma of audience, by the question of just who their poetry is *for*—is it for those interested in formalist poetic experiments, in "avant-garde" or "formally innovative" poets, or is it for the readers who identify with particular forms of political and racial community, with African American or minority poets "of color"? Through the shifts in tone, language, and register from *Tree Tall Woman*, her first collection of poems, to the Stein-inflected *Trimmings* and *S*PeRM**K*T*, to the distinctive Black voice of *Muse & Drudge*, and then to the polyvalent, allusively proliferating, and identity-promiscuous *Sleeping with the Dictionary*, Mullen has courted a diverse audience. But she has also refused consistently to embrace a poetic coterie. Her poems cannot easily be pegged towards pleasing a distinct audience whose existence is marked commercially by anthologies, prizes, and representative presses (though she has also been successful by most measures on all these fronts); nor has she been incorporated critically within particular theoretical and disciplinary frameworks.[2]

That the critical and poetic establishment—from bookstores and poetry readings to reviews and scholarly essays—has admired Mullen's work but also struggled to place it in pre-existing categories raises crucial questions about who gets to write and write *about* various kind of poetry. Most of Mullen's critics have been invested in her as that unlikeliest of poets—a "formally innovative" African American woman writer, one who invites boundary crossings, but who also asserts the distinctiveness of her own identities; a poet who thinks deeply about the politics of (multiple) communities, embraces the recent history of black aesthetics, but who also resists racial essentialisms. As early as 1996, Mullen herself wrote scathingly of the persistence of "aesthetic apartheid" produced by the critical desire to categorize writers and place their work in "the proper critical cubbyhole."[3] If Elisabeth Frost and Claudia Rankine (each coming from distinct and different critical positions) place Mullen alongside groundbreaking American women poets in the twenty-first century, Anthony Reed in his important study of black experimental writing in *Freedom Time* places Mullen alongside Suzan-Lori Parks as a "postlyric" crafter of a "blues poetics."[4] In each of these cases, Mullen's cross-cutting identities—black, female, avant-garde, feminist—collide against and interrogate familiar critical frameworks. Are there other ways, then, to approach her poetry rather than through the question of her contemporary audiences?

"About one-third of my pleasure as a writer," muses Mullen, "comes from the work itself, the process of writing, a third from the response of my contemporaries, and another third in contemplating unknown readers who inhabit a future I will not live to see . . . I try to leave room for unknown readers I can only imagine."[5] In this short essay, "Imagining the Unimagined Reader: Writing to the Unborn and Including the Excluded," Mullen meditates on what it might mean to think of audiences beyond one's immediate local present, to have been the reader who was "unimagined" by prior authors, and to try to imagine many "others," like and unlike herself, who might find and engage with her poems. Her poetic thought experiment with its commitment to forging a "diverse audience" (a key term to which Mullen comes back across various essays and interviews) invites us to consider how her "process of writing" shapes these audiences across space and time. Mullen speaks not only to unknown future readers and critics, but also back to poetic predecessors and forward to would-be poets. The dense texture of literary allusion in her verse—from Callimachus and Sappho to Shakespeare, Stein, and Bessie Smith (among so many others)—gestures towards a very different kind of audience, that of a transhistorical, transnational tradition of lyric poetry.

To broach the question of lyric in the context of Mullen's poetry and of contemporary Black poetics in general is, however, to enter fraught critical terrain. A paradoxical literary object, the lyric poem is radically particular—speaking in a distinct first-person voice, rooted in specific contexts—even as it makes claims to the universal, speaking in and of timeless themes that defy historical contingencies.[6] For minority poets in the contemporary Anglo-European world, that claim to a universal humanity is inseparable from long histories of slavery and colonialism which have aligned such abstracted notions of the human across space and time with forms of whiteness and masculinity.[7] Unsurprisingly, lyric's long history of invoking universal timelessness has thus itself become implicated in the postwar politics of identity formation: Does the lyric index collective desires and a communal politics, or does a vision of the lyric as the expression of a heroic individual subjectivity stand against the pressure of majoritarian concerns? Adorno's influential description of the lyric poem as "refusing to submit to anything heteronomous and constituting itself solely in accordance with its own laws," thereby manifesting a "protest . . . [which] expresses the dream of a world in which things would be different," effectively severed the lyric from its socio-political matrix and argued for its value as a form of art unbound from the material conditions of the world.[8] At the same time, Adorno's extended embrace of a Romantic reimagining of lyric singularity also prompted the question, particularly in American contexts, of whether the lyric itself was a category and term overly complicit in post-Romantic Anglo-European hegemonies. Was lyric something to be rejected and superseded—and if so, how?

Recent scholarship has sought to demystify the lyric's claims to social and cultural centrality by disclosing its fictions of voice and address as no more than the product of lyricization, a process that has elided historical specificity and endorsed the problematic homogenization of various poetic forms and modes under a single monolithic term.[9] In a parallel move, Dorothy Wang, invoking Mullen's early analysis, has called out the separation between a culturally revered, seemingly unraced lyric poetics, that is produced by (mostly) white bodies and unmarked by visible racial experience, and the poetry of so-called minority writers, which is relegated to a sphere of its own. And yet, as Reed's nuanced and sensitive account of Black experimental writing suggests, the pull of lyric—understood as a literary strategy, a techne, and a theoretical node for explorations of voice and subjective expression (however variously conceived)—is inescapable in any consideration of poems that take on and traffic in its fictions.[10] This persistence of lyric as a submerged bass note is especially significant for Mullen's poetry, because of its early engagement with Language poetry (which typically turned away from claims of lyric subjectivity) and its subsequent embrace of one of the lyric's many origin stories in the doubling of Sappho/Sapphire in *Muse & Drudge*.

Mullen speaks somewhat ruefully about her own poetic relation to the lyric, noting that the conceit of "Sappho ... singing the blues" allowed her "to investigate my own connections with this tradition, which was actually called into question by people like the Language poets, who feel that the lyric poem is too much entangled with a subject they want to deconstruct. I have a certain attachment to the lyric subject, but the lyric subject in this poem is multiple not singular."[11] Elsewhere, Mullen has commented on the ironic historical disjuncture between the academic turn to "deconstructing the subject" and the parallel discovery of subjectivity as the ground for a new politics by feminists and people of color: "I had to think about how this discussion of the subject would apply to me."[12] Much has been written about the feminist poetics of *Muse & Drudge* with its frictive link to Sappho, who has come to emblematize female (and often feminist) lyric voice. But in her meditations on lyric and subjectivity, Mullen has also taken aim at perhaps the foremost text of the Anglophone lyric canon—Shakespeare's *Sonnets*. And it is Shakespeare who offers another, slanted perspective on Mullen's relationship to both lyric tradition and feminist poetry.

Almost hidden amid the multiple voices and tonalities of *Muse & Drudge* is a sly imitation of Shakespeare's sonnets #135 and #136, poems which famously and furiously play on the author's name (Will):

> marry at a hotel, annul 'em
> nary hep male rose sullen
> let alley roam, yell melon
> dull normal fellow hammers omelette[13]

Constructed as anagrams and echoes of Harryette Romell Mullen, these lines carry a double charge. In their playful inscription of a poetic signature into a quatrain they mimic a well-worn lyric trope, which Mullen herself traces to Shakespeare and the ghazal.[14] But the Shakespearean reference runs deeper than the mere surface analogy: the play on "Will" (the author) and will (intention, desire, agency) in the sonnets chronicles the dissolution of the speaker as a stable subject within the space of the lyric:

> Wilt thou, whose will is large and spacious,
> Not once vouchsafe to hide my will in thine?

> Shall will in others seem right gracious,
> And in my will no fair acceptance shine?
>
> (#135)

> Swear to thy blind soul that I was thy Will,
> And will, thy soul knows, is admitted there;
> Thus far for love, my love-suit, sweet, fulfil.
> Will, will fulfil the treasure of thy love,
> Ay, fill it full with wills, and my will one.
>
> (#136)[15]

In #135, the speaking "I" and the addressee "thou" interpenetrate emotionally and sexually as the verb ("wilt") merges into the beloved's "will" within which the speaker wants to "hide my will" in a series of bawdy puns. The author's name and intention (Will/will), as many critics have observed, is reduced to the physicality of his desire (will as penis), an ironic diminution that strips the lyric of lofty claims of self-assertion. And in #136, the word "will" is leached of any stable referent at all through a diffusion of sound in the punning, phonic riffing on *will* / *fulfil* / *fill* / *full*. Grammar here barely holds the poem together—the halting modulation of "far for love, my love-suit, sweet, fulfil" is almost "para-grammatic," to use an adjective that the critic Marjorie Perloff has applied to the opening lines of Mullen's *Muse & Drudge*.[16]

Though Mullen never explicitly cites Shakespeare, the affinities between the lyric fragment "[marry at a hotel, annul 'em]" with its diffusion of Mullen's name into phonic analogues (*annul 'em* / *sullen* / *melon* or *marry* / *nary* / *alley*), its subsequent bawdy jokes ("Osiris's irises / his splendid mistress / is his sis Isis"), and delight in scatting ("creole cocoa loca," "fetish coquettish"), re-enact and exceed Shakespearean poetic moves. But even in this, Mullen is ironically knowing—the poem ends with a scene of unrequited, pornographic desire perhaps for the brown (creole?) woman evoked in the earlier lines as "a voyeur leers / at X-rated reels." Here, Mullen seems to wink at the Dark Lady of Shakespeare's sonnets, constructing a racially explicit set of afterlives for the lyric beloved. But the twist is even sharper: the Dark Lady herself speaks teasingly, knowingly, of the unspooling desire for brown bodies (the inversion of *leer/reel* gestures towards this at a linguistic level). The anagrammatic poetic signature that opens this fragment reminds us that Mullen, the poet, both is and is not Sapphire, who, in turn, both is and is not a descendent of Shakespearean Dark Ladies.

It is hardly surprising then that Mullen returns explicitly to Shakespeare's Dark Lady in two different iterations in *Sleeping with the Dictionary*. The poem she targets is the iconic 'Sonnet 130', "My mistress eyes are nothing like the sun," a reverse blazon that parodies both the genre and the kind of muse-beloved it celebrates. The mistress here is dark-haired and possibly dark-skinned ("her breasts are dun"), far from the ethereal, blonde, fair-skinned and rosy-cheeked beauties of Petrarchan cliché. "I grant I never saw a goddess go," quips the poet in plodding iambs, winking towards Petrarch's exaggerated praise of Laura, who is famously compared to Venus through a Virgilian intertext; his lady, when she walks, "treads on the ground." This monosyllabic, metrical Anglo-Saxon groundedness itself enacts a poetic polemic: it linguistically separates the Shakespearean lyric from its classical and Italianate predecessors, brutally rejecting the idealizing erotic dynamics of a popular but somewhat dated tradition in favor of plain speaking. In writing a lyric send-up of lyric excess, Shakespeare thus has it both ways—this is a perfect sonnet, but one that mocks sonneteering—in contemporary terms, he crafts a lyric that claims to be post-lyric.

Mullen's attraction to the ironies condensed into this poem, as well as to its gleeful, simultaneous rejection of *and* inclusion in a lyric tradition that explores erotic subjectivity is easy to understand. In "Variation on a Theme Park" and "Dim Lady" she explores two different critical tendencies in the Shakespearean text while deriving new poems through a set of poetic exercises based on the Oulipo S+7 game.[17] By following a distinctive logic of substitution in each case, Mullen meditates first on the lyric entanglement between the poet and his subject/object (in "Variation") and then on the feminist politics of love poetry (in "Dim Lady"). The diptych thus adds to the transhistorical literary conversations that take shape in the volume as a whole.

Occurring second, "Variation on a Theme Park" is almost a sustained allegory of the history of lyric, especially the sonnet, itself a kind of theme park of literary tropes, fictions, moves. If the contemporary Disney theme park is a commercialized rehashing of familiar fairytale or cartoon narratives and characters that are literalized in rides and shows, so too perhaps is a certain kind of lyric poem which traffics in the slippage between the literal and the metaphoric. Mullen has noted that her substitutions for nouns in Shakespeare's poem are not entirely random but are "free associations" governed by constraint.[18] The poem in fact sets up a distinctive parallel structure of comparison: in the opening lines, "mistress" becomes "Mickey Mouse," "cheek" becomes "checkbook," "lips red" becomes "lyric riddles." Alphabetic order is the logic that ostensibly undergirds Mullen's new text, but it is strategic, acting as a playful critical gloss on Shakespeare, just as Shakespeare had himself glossed Petrarch. Here, the dynamic of Petrarchan love lyric, in which the speaker-lover is hopelessly dependent upon his muse-beloved for his voice and poetic agency, is doubled by and contrasted to Walt Disney's creation of Mickey Mouse as a muse/character with which he has (also) become thoroughly enmeshed. And even the glimmer of lyric delight that Shakespeare retains is firmly quashed by Mullen: "in some perfumes is there more delight / Than in the breath that from my mistress reeks" becomes "in some purchases there is more deliberation than in the bargains that my Mickey Mouse redeems." But this too is a distinctively Shakespearean deflation: love, money, and career advancement are inextricable metaphors for each other in the *Sonnets* as the lover repeatedly weighs the costs of and returns on his desire.[19]

The so-called Dark Lady poems are famous in fact for their corrosive view of love and sexual disgust ("The expense of spirit in a waste of shame / Is lust in action"). The mistress has been dubbed the "Dark Lady" by generations of critics for her infidelity, her possible promiscuity, and her supposed depravity, thereby collapsing her appearance with moral essence—a move that Kim Hall has identified as a racializing trope widely exploited in early modern literature.[20] Mullen is alert to this intersection of racial and gender normativity in Shakespeare's poem and mocks it through strategic substitution. "Black wires" become "blond Wonder Bras"; "roses damasked, red and white" becomes "roadkill damaged, riddled and wintergreen"; and "Goddess go" becomes "googolplex groan." These juxtapositions become a feminist commentary on the simultaneous idealization and demonization of women in love lyric, which subjects them to the constrictions of normative beauty and behavior only to reject them violently. In this kind of world, love cannot but dissolve into loneliness; the beloved is about as precious ("rare") as "any souvenir bought with free coupons." We are not far from the biting critique of *Muse & Drudge*.

"Dim Lady" amplifies these themes by abandoning the substitutive logic of alphabetic order for analogical association and returning to the idiom of *S*PeRM**K*T*. 'Sonnet 130' now indexes the commodification of women as domestic cleaning products ("Liquid Paper," "her mop were Slinkys," "minty-fresh mouthwashes") and cheap food (Red Lobster, Shakey's Pizza Parlors, "garlic breeze," "scrumptious twinkie"). Going beyond the Shakespearean pretext and deflating the poetic register even further, Mullen meditates on gender and class politics through her choice of endearments ("honeybunch," "main squeeze") and an almost aggressively plain-speaking blazon (peepers, kisser, racks, noggin, mug). Mullen even replicates Shakespeare's rhymes and iambs, only to replace them with contemporary signifiers that perfectly modulate the lyric beloved into a pin-up movie star ("I grant I never saw a goddess go" is transformed into the inspired "I don't know any Marilyn Monroes").

Unlike "Variations" which engages in an extended metaphoric commentary on the terms of 'Sonnet 130', "Dim Lady" more straightforwardly discloses the structure of substitution as a poetic and critical device. "What's so striking

... about S+7," observes Mullen, "is the durability of grammatical and linguistic structures ... the words substituted, however arbitrary, nonsensical, and meaningless, add layers of poetic texture, potential metaphor and meaning to the text. In this manner, whatever is lost of the original is supplemented and enriched by what is substituted in its place."[21] I would argue that in Mullen's instantiations of this process, there is not "loss" but rather obscured recall as Mullen now hails the poem's suppressed subject—that is, sexual desire for a woman separated from the lover by the social (and poetic) constructs of race and class.

Taken together, however, these poems are more than just refractions of Shakespeare, or virtuoso emblems of Mullen's poetic play. They are also Oulipian interventions and disruptions of literary history and genre. Mullen has commented repeatedly on these poems' emergence from her attraction to Oulipo writers and techniques for their "systematic effort to demystify the poetic process."[22] "They dispense with the ancient mythology of the poet inspired by the muse, in favor of games, devices, constraints, procedures, and experiments that might result in works of 'potential literature,'" she has said.[23] This striking contrast seems to pit a hoary lyric tradition against the radical openness of postmodern, experimentalist poetry, whose investment in language games seems to dispense with the subjective communion of poet and muse. But, as Mullen undoubtedly is aware, the contrast she sets up here is one most commonly associated with Romantic and modernist accounts of lyric—a well-worn critical trope that her own poetry seeks to leave behind. The Oulipo practices, in which she delights, reach back, in fact, to older, early modern and classical modes of lyric praxis, paradoxically allowing Mullen to explore alternative historical traditions of lyric self-consciousness.

Mullen had already invoked an older tradition of lyric in *Muse & Drudge*, not only through the persona of Sappho/Sapphire, but in the epigram from Callimachus: "Fatten your animal for sacrifice, poet, but keep your muse slender." These lines, drawn from Diane Rayor's translation of the Prologue to the *Aetia*, a poem now only known in fragments, open an inset passage that celebrates lyric's superiority over other forms in terms that are playful and ironic.[24] In a series of contrasts between ponderous long poems (epic) and the slender brevity of the short poem (lyric), Callimachus ventriloquizes Apollo's command to him to write poems in a distinctive form: slim, delicate, unexpected, unusual.[25] The contrast between the fat sheep and the slender muse is a teasing contrast between the most familiar tropes of Homeric epic (which frequently describes animal sacrifice) and elegy/lyric (whose Muse-beloved is slender, beautiful, and frequently unattainable). Already for Callimachus, writing around 270 BCE, these poetic fictions are legible as such; lyric's association with cicadas, dewdrops, and the intricacy of the miniature artifact foregrounds the short poem's particular, extraordinary craftsmanship.[26]

In *Sleeping with the Dictionary*, Oulipo techniques enable Mullen to highlight this kind of self-reflexive craftsmanship with regard to remakings and reinterpretations of Shakespeare's *Sonnets*, producing poems that in turn participate in a long tradition of lyric poems *about* lyric poetics. For though Mullen's variations on Shakespeare have often been read as kind of "writing back" to a white canon, a strategy of resistance and supersession, the poem she chooses to "recycle," 'Sonnet 130', is already a parody, a recycled send-up of Petrarchan tropes and the fantasy of a particular kind of lyric address—itself a reworking of the very classical tropes that Mullen herself invokes in *Muse & Drudge*.[27] Like Sappho and Callimachus, Shakespeare indexes a canonical account of lyric, but it is—perhaps surprisingly—not one that fetishizes poetic inspiration and the singularity of literary genius. Instead, it is a vision of lyric as poetic play.

Shakespeare himself drew on well-known games of poetic constraint and imitation (*imitatio*), the humanist term that resonates powerfully with Mullen's notion of literary "recycling." Humanist *imitatio*, the practice of bringing ancient, exemplary texts into one's own literary craft was not merely an intertextual strategy, or a kind of slavish homage to the canon.

467

Instead, Renaissance writers understood *imitatio* as a creative act of imaginative (re)making, as a textual bridge between the cultural and historical discontinuities of their (modern) present and a (classical) past. Such literary revision required a delicate balancing act—part homage, part supersession, it invited the fusion of veneration with irreverence.[28] When Mullen writes in the preface to *Recyclopedia* that "poetry . . . remakes and renews words, images, and ideas, transforming surplus cultural information into something unexpected," she writes against post-Romantic accounts of lyric, describing instead an early modern poetic craft that would have been intuitive to Shakespeare and his contemporaries.[29]

For contemporary poets like Mullen, Shakespeare has of course become the classical past whose fragments must be shored up and remade as the foundations of our own future. But for feminist women writers, Shakespeare is an especially complex emblem. Following Virginia Woolf's *A Room of One's Own*, which imagines the hypothetical life of Shakespeare's sister, "Shakespeare" has come to name a literary system whose patriarchal values excluded women from literary careers and canonical status. But at the same time, Shakespeare, the consummate recycler, is also an enabler—the poet who saves some of his most powerful verse for female characters (Juliet, Viola, Portia, Cleopatra), whose Dark Lady seems to wrestle for control within the space of the sonnets. Writing in 1971 about women writers' need to "re-vision" literary and patriarchal pasts, Adrienne Rich notes that "Re-vision—the act of looking back, of seeing with fresh eyes, of entering an old text from a new critical direction—is for us more than a chapter in cultural history: it is an act of survival."[30] For Rich, too, the poetic idol to supersede is Shakespeare. With a racialized ignorance that is palpable now—Rich suggests that to achieve this supersession women must move beyond the mode of "the blues song: a cry of pain, of victimization, or a lyric of seduction," to embrace their anger and forge poems "out of a newly released courage to name, to love each other, to share risk and grief and celebration."[31]

It is perhaps no surprise that Mullen, whose poetic alter ego unabashedly "sings the blues" is also the poet who "re-visions" not only Shakespeare but also Rich and a long tradition of feminist entanglements with his poetry. In the long autobiographical prose poem, "She Swam On from Sea to Shine," Mullen revises Rich's iconic feminist poem, "Diving into the Wreck," by triangulating it with the Shine tale (from the well-known African American toast) and with Shakespeare:

> When the ship went down, she wouldn't sink, had to swim, she brought her suit ... From sea to shine, she swam on. The whales sang Celtic music, dolphins frisked her. She was worked over and under she let her mind wander. Let it roll and keep on rolling on and on. Revolution is a cycle that never ends. Rumors of May made mermaids murmur. Plato opens utopia to poets on opiates.[32]

The allusive density of this passage, its teasing wordplay, puns, and brilliant anagrammatic closure, hover between narrative and lyric. In this final movement, Mullen explicitly looks back to Rich. But instead of diving curiously into an old wreck (of history, of consciousness), Mullen's protagonist escapes a wreck-in-the-making, leaving it behind in an act of liberation that transforms her into a survivor who discovers new worlds. She is not, like Rich's lyric speaker, a seeker of old myths, an explorer and witness "who came to see the damage that was done." Instead, she is a poetic agent who swims alongside whales and dolphins, a maker of revolutions both literal and symbolic.

The intertext that punctuates this transformation from Rich's static exploration of a dead, encrusted object into Mullen's agentive, exuberant poetic discoverer is Shakespeare's *A Midsummer Night's Dream*:

> Thou rememberest
> Since once I sat upon a promontory,
> And heard a mermaid on a dolphin's back
> Uttering such dulcet and harmonious breath

> That the rude sea grew civil at her song
> And certain stars shot madly from their spheres,
> To hear the sea-maid's music.[33]

These lines are spoken by the fairy king Oberon who, recently rejected by Titania, recalls for Puck a failed attempt by Cupid to inflame a "fair vestal" with erotic passion. It is a tale of female resistance to male desire, and of the power of unfettered female song—figured by the singing mermaid on the dolphin's back—which calms the rage of the natural world and fills it with pleasure. Mullen's prose-poem contains a distilled memory of these lines condensed into a commentary on female poetic agency. Swimming among the dolphins, singing whales, and murmuring mermaids who hear "Rumors of May" (of the revolutions of May 1968 perhaps), Mullen's protagonist can dream of utopian possibilities that only poets disclose.

Notes

1. See interviews collected in Harryette Romell Mullen, *The Cracks between What We Are and What We Are Supposed to Be: Essays and Interviews* (Tuscaloosa: University of Alabama Press, 2012). For Crumpacker see: https://poets.org/text/licked -all-over-english-language-harryette-mullen-conversation
2. On these challenges of critically categorizing Mullen's poetry, see Anthony Reed, *Freedom Time: The Poetics and Politics of Black Experimental Writing* (Baltimore, MD: Johns Hopkins University Press, 2014).
3. Harryette Mullen, "Poetry and Identity" in *The Cracks between What We Are and What We Are Supposed to Be*, 12.
4. See Elisabeth Frost and Cynthia Hogue, eds., *Innovative Women Poets: An Anthology of Contemporary Poetry and Interviews* (Iowa City: University of Iowa Press, 2006); Claudia Rankine and Juliana Spahr, eds., *American Women Poets in the 21st Century: Where Lyric Meets Language* (Middletown, CT: Wesleyan University Press, 2013); and Reed, *Freedom Time*, 23.

5. Mullen, *The Cracks between What We Are and What We Are Supposed to Be*, 3.

6. The question of what "lyric" is—as a literary and critical category—is a deeply fraught one. A sample of the current debates are available in Virginia Jackson and Yopie Prins, eds., *The Lyric Theory Reader: A Critical Anthology* (Baltimore, MD: Johns Hopkins University Press, 2014); and Jonathan D. Culler, *Theory of the Lyric* (Cambridge, MA: Harvard University Press, 2015). Reed, *Freedom Time*, summarizes relevant aspects of the debate for contemporary Black poetry. I draw here on my own work on the long histories of lyric in the classical and early modern periods.

7. For the imbrications of "universal humanity" and humanism with slavery and colonialism see Sylvia Wynter's now-seminal essay, "Unsettling the Coloniality of Being/Power/Truth/Freedom: Towards the Human, After Man, Its Overrepresentation—An Argument," *CR: The New Centennial Review* 3, no. 3 (2003): 257–337.

8. Theodor W. Adorno, "On Lyric Poetry and Society," in *Notes to Literature*, ed. Rolf Tiedemann, trans. Shierry Weber Nicholsen (New York: Columbia University Press, 1992), 40.

9. See Virginia Jackson, *Dickinson's Misery: A Theory of Lyric Reading* (Princeton, NJ: Princeton University Press, 2005) and also alternate claims for lyric's social politics as in Oren Izenberg, *Being Numerous: Poetry and the Ground of Social Life*, 20/21 (Princeton, NJ: Princeton University Press, 2011).

10. See, for instance, the recuperation of lyric as a useful critical term in Reed, *Freedom Time* and Sonya Posmentier, *Cultivation and Catastrophe: The Lyric Ecology of Modern Black Literature* (Baltimore, MD: Johns Hopkins University Press, 2017).

11. Elisabeth Frost interview with Harryette Mullen, in Frost and Hogue, *Innovative Women Poets*, 199.

12. Mullen, *The Cracks between What We Are and What We Are Supposed to Be*, 239.

13. Mullen, from *Muse & Drudge* in *Recyclopedia*, 162.

14. Mullen, *The Cracks between What We Are and What We Are Supposed to Be*, 209.

15. Cited from William Shakespeare, *Shakespeare's Sonnets*, ed. Stephen Booth (New Haven, CT: Yale University Press, 1994).

16. Marjorie Perloff, "After Language Poetry: Innovation and Its Theoretical Discontents," *Contemporary Poetics* (2007): 15–38.
17. Harryette Mullen, *Sleeping with the Dictionary* (Berkeley: University of California Press, 2002). On the genesis of these poems, see Mullen, *The Cracks between What We Are and What We Are Supposed to Be*, 211.
18. Ibid.
19. Examples of this abound across the plays and sonnets: to take just one example, see 'Sonnet 142', where the poet accuses the Dark Lady of sealing "false bonds of love as oft as mine / Robbed others' beds' revenues of their rents."
20. Kim F. Hall, "'These Bastard Signs of Fair': Literary Whiteness in Shakespeare's Sonnets," in *Post-Colonial Shakespeares* (Routledge, 1998).
21. Mullen, *The Cracks between What We Are and What We Are Supposed to Be*, 47.
22. Mullen, *The Cracks between What We Are and What We Are Supposed to Be*, 207; this is echoed almost verbatim in the Crumpacker interview.
23. See: https://poets.org/text/licked-all-over-english-language-harr yette-mullen-conversation
24. It is important to note that Callimachus' commentary in the Prologue to the *Aetia* does not specifically invoke "lyric" per se but has been taken to refer to elegiac (and thus lyric) poetry. See Benjamin Acosta-Hughes and Susan A. Stephens, "Callimachean 'Lyric,'" *Trends in Classics* 9, no. 2 (November 15, 2017): 226–247.
25. See the translation consulted by Mullen: Diane J. Rayor and William W. Batstone, eds., *Latin Lyric and Elegiac Poetry: An Anthology of New Translations* (New York: Garland Publishing, 1995).
26. For Mullen there is also something ironic about the fusion of sacrificial sheep and slender muse in the figure of the (not-slender) Sapphire.
27. This point is also made, though with different stakes, in Vincent Broqua, "Living-with Shakespeare?" *Transatlantica. Revue d'études américaines. American Studies Journal*, no. 1 (June 22, 2010).
28. On these aspects of humanist imitation see the seminal discussion in Thomas M. Greene, *The Light in Troy: Imitation*

and Discovery in Renaissance Poetry (New Haven, CT: Yale University Press, 1982).

29. Harryette Mullen, *Recyclopedia: Trimmings, S*PeRM**K*T, and Muse & Drudge* (St. Paul, MN: Graywolf Press, 2006), vii.

30. Adrienne Rich, *Adrienne Rich's Poetry and Prose*, ed. Albert Gelpi and Barbara Charlesworth Gelpi (New York: W.W. Norton, 1993), 167. Mullen recalls listening to Rich read in an interview with Hogue; see Mullen, *The Cracks between What We Are and What We Are Supposed to Be*, 238.

31. Rich, *Adrienne Rich's Poetry and Prose*, 176. Rich would later write that she did not know of the tradition of Bessie Smith "When I dreamed that dream, was I wholly ignorant of the tradition of Bessie Smith and other women's blues lyrics which transcended victimization to sing of resistance and independence?" (note 3 in this edition).

32. Mullen, *Sleeping with the Dictionary*, 66.

33. *A Midsummer Night's Dream*, 2.1. Cited from William Shakespeare, *The Riverside Shakespeare*, ed. G. Blakemore Evans and J.J.M. Tobin (New York: Houghton Mifflin, 1997).

"Native or Not" – On Harryette Mullen's Tanka Diary

Daniel Kane

Harryette Mullen's *Urban Tumbleweed: Notes from a Tanka Diary*[1] opens with two epigraphs that set the tone for Mullen's own series of short, three-line poems focused on noting the dissonances and harmonies between the urban and the natural. The first is a haiku from Richard Wright, the author of *Native Son* and *Black Boy* – "Keep straight down this block, / then turn right where you will find / a peach tree blooming." The second is from scientist and agronomist George Washington Carver – "Look about you. Take hold of the things that / are here. Let them talk to you."[2] Seeing how she yokes the sciences and humanities together while aligning herself to transformative black figures, readers of Mullen's book might expect a work that adapts the tanka to address clearly race-based concerns. Indeed, if readers were to actually skip the poems themselves and jump straight to the "Acknowledgments" section at the end of the book, they would find a thank you from Mullen to Camille T. Dungy who, Mullen informs us:

> chose one of my poems for *Black Nature: Four Centuries of African American Nature Poetry*.[3] In an anthology that includes haiku by Richard Wright, Dungy contests the boundaries of nature poetry as well as African American poetry, resisting typical assumptions that "green" is white and "urban" is black.[4]

No surprise here, perhaps, given Mullen is at this point in time one of the most renowned Black poets in North America and Europe and that her work has explored "the boundaries of ... African American poetry" consistently. While *Urban Tumbleweed* rarely invokes the kinds of "voice-based, Black Arts-inspired poetry" in Mullen's debut *Tree Tall Woman*,[5] an informed reader of Mullen's oeuvre who is aware of Mullen's self-conscious manipulation of her works to anticipate, integrate, and shape distinct audiences[6] might understand the book as engaged in conversation with Mullen's earlier books. For example, the visual appearance of *Urban Tumbleweed* – three discrete three-line tankas on each page – points back to Mullen's *Muse & Drudge*, in which four quatrains fill each page, thus inviting the reader to make connections across the texts. The fact that *Urban Tumbleweed* adapts a prescribed form also points back to Mullen's experiments with restraint-based forms in *Sleeping with the Dictionary*. *Urban Tumbleweed* is an important extension of Mullen's play with her audiences' expectations of how poetry produced by Black writers can and should reveal itself at the level of diction and form. And yet, as this essay will show, there is much that is entirely new in *Urban Tumbleweed*, both in terms of what it brings into Mullen's project – a relatively straightforward urban pastoral mode, an adaptation of a relatively ancient poetic form – and what it leaves out.

Consciously Constructing a "Black Voice"

African American "identity," Mullen explains:

> is as much an aspect of the work as a concern with language, poetics, and form. I think this is evident in all of my work, whether I was consciously constructing a "black voice" or "black literary style" in my first book, *Tree Tall Woman*; writing "the new sentence" in *Trimmings* and *S*PeRM**K*T*; experimenting with kinky quatrains in *Muse & Drudge*; or playing Oulipo word games with my

American Heritage in [. . .] *Sleeping with the Dictionary* [. . .]
We often tend to reduce and simplify black expressive tradi-
tions, and we must acknowledge the diversity and hybridity
of those traditions.[7]

Taking into account the interrelated themes and concerns that
Mullen proposes link all her works, it would be reasonable
for a reader to ask how *Urban Tumbleweed* acknowledges
– or rather, *whether* it acknowledges – "the diversity and
hybridity" of black expressive traditions. This is a particu-
larly pressing question given that the form Mullen chooses
to adapt in *Urban Tumbleweed* is the tanka. Produced origi-
nally in seventh century Japan, the tanka was divided into five
lines determined by a syllabic count of, respectively, 5 / 7 / 5 /
7 / 7. The tanka is often compared to the sonnet because there
is a shift or *volta* in the third line that serves to move from the
depiction of an image to a delineation of the poet's emotional
response. Tanka, while often pointing to the poet's relation-
ship to the natural world, also expressed lovers' intimate
feelings and desires. Take, for example, Kenneth Rexroth's
translation of Yosano Akiko's tanka:

> Black hair
> Tangled in a thousand strands.
> Tangled my hair and
> Tangled my tangled memories
> Of our long nights of love making.[8]

Beginning with an image of tangled black hair, this tanka
continues according to plan by turning at the third line to
draw a metaphor between the tangled hair and the ardor-
filled if complex sensuous memories of the speaker-lover.

In light of the tanka's history, then, it seems initially that
there is little connection between Mullen's three-line tankas
and the Japanese five-line tanka. Visually speaking, Mullen's
poems point to the three-line haiku more immediately than
they do the tanka. In terms of narrative content, Mullen's
urban pastoral mode is arguably more attuned to the haiku's
depiction of the poet's relationship to and visions of nature

than it is to the tanka's expression of carnal and romantic feeling. And yet, Mullen in the preface to the book makes no mention of a beloved and sexualized other who an informed reader might expect to be at the very least implicitly invoked in a book framed as a "tanka diary." Instead, Mullen provides readers with a biographical frame through which to read the diary as an imaginative exercise in addressing the cliché association of the poet's privileged relationship to the natural environment:

> Each outing, however brief, becomes an occasion for reflection. Los Angeles, however urban, offers everyday encounters with nature.
> So I began the diary despite being able to recognize only the most common creatures, and feeling that I lack a proper lexicon to write about the natural world, when what we call natural or native is more than ever open to question.[9]

Mullen here rather cheerfully acknowledges the "lack [of] a proper lexicon" revealing the poet's fundamental disconnect from the nomenclature of nature as – given the context of the afterword and her work as a whole – she hints towards an elastic and fundamentally anti-essentialist view of race ("what we call natural or native"). As Mullen writes at the end of the preface, "What of a poet who does not know the proper names of native and non-native fauna and flora, who sees 'a yellow flower by the creek' – not a *Mimulus*?" Readers, given the aura Carver and Wright generate over the book by virtue of the epigraphs, and perhaps informed by their readings of Mullen's other works, might be forgiven for looking forward to a book that, as Rebecca Hamilton argues, "illuminates environmental damage and systemic inequalities based on class and race, ultimately modeling how a sharpened awareness of body and place cultivates attention to broader social and ecological realities."[10]

And yet, given the paucity of recognizably African American vernacular language we actually find in *Urban Tumbleweed*, especially compared to Mullen's earlier works, I wonder how much readers such as Hamilton impose preconceived expectations about how "race" can and should resonate in Mullen's writing. After all, while there are certainly instances throughout the book that dramatize the unequal effects of environmental degradation on working-class and poor subjects, there is little in the way of explicit references to "inequalities based on . . . race" itself. In a book stretching to 122 pages containing 366 tankas, we should at the very least note that there are only five or six moments in the book that might illustrate overtly Mullen's efforts to resist "typical assumptions that 'green' is white and 'urban' is black."

The first is "This curly cloud don't grow straight or need / straightening. It takes rough wind to wreck the 'do.' / To some, when brushed and combed it still looks tangled." Writing "don't" instead of "doesn't," Mullen here conjugates the auxiliary verb in a manner typical of African American vernacular English in order to assist the reader in understanding the "curly cloud" as a metaphor for an Afro hair "do." I emphasize the singularity of this moment in part because no other book of Mullen's features so *few* direct evocations of African American dialect or, indeed, African American culture considered broadly.

Later, Mullen references "Svartmangatan" simply to point out that the eponymous Stockholm street "wasn't named / for a black man, but for a man dressed in black."[11] In a subsequent tanka the reader learns of a friend "visiting with us in Los Angeles" who "went out for a sunny walk, returned / with wrists bound, misapprehended by cops."[12] Given Mullen's choice to not provide us with more detail, one can only speculate here whether the "friend" was yet another person caught up in the dragnet of walking while Black, or whether, *as readers*, we are perhaps too quick to automatically make that assumption. A later tanka describes the speaker gathering strands of her own hair and rolling them "into a thick Ziggy dreadlock; / mail to an artist who collects the hair of poets."[13] Then, near the end of *Urban Tanka*, Mullen asks the reader, "Remember that song about possum up / a 'simmon tree? That's who's living in your / backyard, opossum up the persimmon tree."[14]

This final reference to a specifically black cultural form is fascinating given Mullen turns "possum up a 'simmon tree" into the standard English phrase "opossum up the persimmon tree." Why, one wonders, does Mullen choose to invoke a song *The Journal of American Folklore* identifies as "From Eastern North Carolina; negroes; MS. Of W.O Scroggs"[15] only to replace the "'simmon" with the standard English "persimmon"? Why did she omit the apostrophe one expects preceding "possum"? Mullen's omissions and revisions in this tanka are similar to the way Mullen omits apostrophes in her early poem "The Joy" (included in her book *Blues Baby*[16]) to distance herself "from the tradition of blues poetry" and to call "attention to the intersection of idiomatic and accepted English . . . by refusing the expected apostrophe."[17] Mullen sets up a kind of tense dialectic between what Antonio Brown calls "Black Speak"[18] and standard written English. Where Brown insists that "Black Speak communicates a 'truth' by infusing its messages with the linguistic style that formulates and informs cultural identities and communities,"[19] Mullen's code-switching tends to push back against the very assumption that there is an inherent truth-value to the inscription of Black oral tradition. Both humorously translating dialect for an implicitly white subject suggested by the pronoun "your" and pushing back against readers' expectations that Mullen herself speaks/writes similarly to the dialect in the title "Possum up the 'Simmon Tree," the tanka reveals "both a suturing to black cultural specificity and a splitting from it."[20]

One tanka stands out for its "suturing" and "splitting." Coming in at exactly the half-way mark in the book (page 61 of 122), we find an almost outrageously bland language employed to refer to collard greens, a vegetable that scholar Loretta Henderson notes is "encoded with blackness":[21]

Mom grew these leafy collards in her organic
garden. She picked them this morning.
Tonight they go well with our cornbread and yams.[22]

If, as Thorsson insists, "it is not just that recipes and food-ways are women's work in a stereotypical sense but that studying formal and thematic uses of food can deepen our understanding of black women's writing,"[23] what is the reader to do with this tanka given that Mullen's references to food in other volumes are aligned much more overtly to interrogating racial categories, celebrating black culture, and the like? One thinks here, for example, of the vicious punning Mullen employs in *Muse & Drudge* to highlight the way poverty is so often criminalized and raced. Take, for example, the stanza "disappeared undocumented workhorse / homeless underclass breeder / dissident pink collard criminal / terminal deviant indigent slut."[24] "Collard" here serves pretty clearly as a homonym for "colored," thus layering the prejudices of a white supremacist, classist, and sexist hegemony on to a stereotypically Black Southern dish. Importantly, Mullen – as she so often does throughout her work – stages intersectional kinship with other subaltern groups here. As Jennifer Reimer reads the stanza:

> Mullen's wordplay *transa*culturates the relationship between African Americans, women from the Global South, and immigrants in the US and encourages us to see continuity between America's classic anti-black rhetoric and today's increasing national hysteria over immigration at the nation's southern border. "Workhorse" invokes slavery and/or the blue-collar labor performed by a so-called underemployed and unskilled black "underclass." Mullen emphasizes the racialized and gendered aspect of work through her reference to a "dissident pink collard criminal." "Pink collard" combines "pink-collar," a common term for women's work, with "collard," as in "collard greens," a food stereotypically associated with Southern black culture(s). Indeed, "dissident" and "criminal," along with "homeless underclass breeder" and "terminal deviant indigent slut," are racist labels used to describe African American women in the urban ghetto.[25]

Reimer's excellent reading makes Mullen's "collard" as it sits and sounds so flatly in the pages of *Urban Tumbleweed* all the weirder. This is particularly the case as even the most experimental or "language-centered" works of Mullen's such as *Trimmings, S*PeRM**K*T*, and *Sleeping with the Dictionary* "rely," as Thorsson rightly puts it, "on a store-house of African forms as much as Mullen's earliest poems do." Thorsson goes far in showing how Mullen "declines aspects of a stereotypical 'authentic [black] voice' even in her earliest poems," insisting Mullen's experiments with "food-ways" enable her to "resist limited notions of racial authen-ticity."[26] Informed by Thorsson, I read *Urban Tumbleweed* as Mullen's most extreme manifestation of the limitations of "racial authenticity" as embodied in written language. Refusing all the more the temptation to fetishize racial iden-tity through the enactment of and play with dialect, *Urban Tumbleweed* stands as perhaps Mullen's most challenging book yet in terms of confronting readers not just about their potential "assumptions that 'green' is white and 'urban' is black" but, going further, their assumptions about what con-stitutes Black voice itself as it is mediated through text.

Urban Tumbleweed: A Love Story?

I opened this essay by pointing out that the tanka historically addressed romantic feeling. The tanka "has always been a poem of feelings, often involving metaphor and other figura-tive language (not generally used in haiku) . . . In the words of Sanford Goldstein, 'behind the scene is the autobiographi-cal moment of the poet.'"[27] Keeping this definition in mind, I want to identify – however tentatively – what I perceive to be Mullen's most interesting engagement with this particular generic aspect of the tanka. I say "tentatively" in all sincerity, as I recall my surprise the first time I read *Urban Tumbleweed* in coming across several references to a "you" and collective "we" and "our" that struck me as ambiguously but sugges-tively tender. Could Mullen be using the tanka to address and describe her own personal relationships? And if so, how does this reflect back on Mullen's decision to employ a lan-guage that marks a departure from her earlier use of African American dialect?

If one focuses on tracking its appearance, the "you" seems to cohere into a figure that, informed as we are by the generic conventions of the tanka, takes on an ever more romantic and domestic cast. The first time a "you" appears that seems to be pointing to a beloved other is framed as follows: "No tree in sight to shade us from the searing / glare, that cloudless day in Chinatown, / you stopped to buy a paper parasol."[28] We are in couples territory here, the "us" presented imagistically – "glare" serves as a spotlight on the two as the "you" buys a "paper parasol." The fragility of the parasol, combined with the vulnerability of the couple exposed to the sun's glare, suggests a kind of impermanence and pathos characterizing the historical tanka. Like the tankas of more conventional poets before her, Mullen's tanka "crystallize(s) a moment of beauty and sadness," and, like "love tanka and nature tanka" is "connected with nature through what might be termed an 'organic metaphor.'"[29]

These aesthetic moves are extended and expanded on in subsequent pages as "you," "we," and "us" are organised around a quasi-narrative that shows a couple ensconced in an idealized and relatively privileged Californian domesticity. *Viz.* "Don't need picket fences, brick wall, / or razor wire. Our home's protected by / prickly pear cactus and thorny bougainvillea";[30] "I have shamelessly neglected all of the succulent / jades and aloes you planted around the patio— / and they have thrived";[31] "When you complain about the worm / in your salad bowl, our server assures us, / 'That is how you know the lettuce is organic'";[32] "Yesterday we talked about your favorite / poem. Today you brought a gift / of fully ripe persimmons in a paper bag";[33] "After hearing that poem from my tanka diary, / you handed me a smooth and pleasing stone / shaped like a lopsided heart."[34]

Of course, the "you" could represent more than one person rather than a specific beloved subject. The "you" at times seems to work as a self-referential second-person address. Alternatively, as Hamilton suggests, the "you" "potentially includes the reader as subject."[35] That said, the presence of recurring images and motifs often suggests a different model. For example, there are a series of references to hiking that serve to bind the "you" all the more to a romantically connected "we" and "our": "We'd planned to hike to the top of the trail / for a breathtaking view of Pacific, / but turned back down at the sight of a rattler";[36] "Clean dirt marks the path, lined with white / stones, winding through the well-tended park, / leading to a rippling stream created for our pleasure";[37] "Hiking up Topanga Canyon trail, / we spoke of bobcats, coyotes, and rattlesnakes— / but only harmless lizards crossed our path";[38] "I'm sure I must have been laughing / the first time we hiked that mountain trail / when you introduced me to the sticky monkey flower."[39] Bookended near the beginning and end by the image of the mountain trail, the implicitly romantic couple serve as a kind of anchor for the otherwise kaleidoscopic (if roughly chronological) form of Mullen's tanka diary.

That Mullen does not describe the features of the "you" – there are no identifying markers of gender, race, or color ascribed to the subject – speaks, I think, to the complicated politics of the book as a whole. As *Urban Tumbleweed* plays within and at the edges of numerous genres and modes, including urban pastoral, travel writing, journalistic reportage, haiku, diary, ecopoem, and walk poem, so Mullen uses the occasion to expand her critique of inequity under capitalism initiated in her first book *Tree Tall Woman* and carried through in every subsequent book through a variety of forms (the "kinky quatrains" of *Muse & Drudge*, the "new sentences" in *Trimmings* and *S*PeRM**K*T*, and the Oulipo-inspired procedural poems in *Sleeping with the Dictionary*). Part of what marks this book as so curiously distinct from preceding works, however, is what is *not* in the poem. "The essentializing of black English as the natural way that black people are supposed to speak," Mullen notifies us, "is problematic for me."[40] The mostly absent "black English" in *Urban Tumbleweed* becomes a kind of positive, productive presence that nudges Mullen's ever growing, ever diverse groups of readers to reflect, focus on, and make strange the interlinked natural, urban, and racial/cultural grounds they travel through. "Native or not," Mullen writes, "you're welcome in our gardens."[41]

Notes

1. Harryette Mullen, *Urban Tumbleweed: Notes from a Tanka Diary* (Graywolf Press, 2013).
2. Ibid., xi.
3. Camille T. Dungy, *Black Nature: Four Centuries of African American Nature Poetry* (University of Georgia Press, 2009).
4. Mullen, *Urban Tumbleweed*, 125.
5. Jessica Lewis Luck, "Entries on a Post-Language Poetics in Harryette Mullen's 'Dictionary,'" *Contemporary Literature* 49, no. 3 (2008), 358.
6. For example, in an interview with Farah Griffin, Michael Magee, and Kristin Gallagher, Mullen explains "one reason I wrote *Muse and Drudge* is because having written *Tree Tall Woman*, when I went around reading from that book there were a lot of black people in my audience. There would be white people and brown people and maybe other people of color as well. Suddenly, when I went around to do readings of *Trimmings* and *S*PeRM**K*T*, I would be the one black person in the room, reading my poetry. I mean I'd find myself in a room that typically had no other people of color in it – which, you know, I could do, and it was interesting. But that's not necessarily what I wanted, and I thought, 'How am I going to get all these folks to sit down together in the same room?' *Muse and Drudge* was my attempt to create that audience. I wanted the different audiences for my various works to come together. I was happy to see those people who were interested in the formal innovation that emerged when I was writing *Trimmings* and *S*PeRM**K*T*, partly because I was responding, in those books, to the work of Gertrude Stein, while dealing with my own concerns around race, gender, and culture. I had been hanging out with the language writers in the Bay Area, and listening to them and reading their work, so there was all of that influence as well. And then I thought, okay, well, I'm going to need to do *something* to integrate this audience, because it felt *uncomfortable* to be the only black person in the room reading

my work to this audience. I mean, it was something that I could do up to a certain point with pure gratitude that an audience existed for my new work. I felt, 'Well, this is interesting. This tells me something about the way that I'm writing now,' although I didn't think I was any less black in those two books or any more black in *Tree Tall Woman*. But I think that the way that these things get defined in the public domain is that, yeah, people saw *S*PeRM**K*T* as being not a *black* book but an *innovative* book. And this idea that you can be black *or* innovative, you know, is what I was really trying to struggle against. And *Muse and Drudge* was my attempt to show that I can do both at the same time." "A conversation with Harryette Mullen," accessed February 12, 2022: http://writing.upenn .edu/epc/authors/mullen/interview-new.html

7. Harryette Mullen, *The Cracks Between What We Are and What We Are Supposed to Be: Essays and Interviews* (University of Alabama Press, 2012), 207.

8. Kenneth Rexroth, *One Hundred More Poems from the Japanese* (New Directions Publishing, 1976), 7.

9. Mullen, *Urban Tumbleweed*, viii.

10. Rebecca Hamilton, "Forms of Attention: Notes from Harryette Mullen's Tanka Diary," *Journal of Modern Literature* 42, no. 1 (2018), 124.

11. Mullen, *Urban Tumbleweed*, 80.

12. Ibid., 94.

13. Ibid., 96.

14. Ibid., 114.

15. E.C. Perrow, "Songs and Rhymes from the South," *The Journal of American Folklore* 26, no. 100 (1913), 131.

16. Harryette Mullen, *Blues Baby: Early Poems* (Bucknell University Press, 2002).

17. Courtney Thorsson, "Foodways in Contemporary African American Poetry: Harryette Mullen and Evie Shockley," *Contemporary Literature* 57, no. 2 (2016), 193.

18. Antonio Brown, "Performing 'Truth': Black Speech Acts," *African American Review* 36, no. 2 (2002), 213–225.

19. Ibid., 213.

20. Erica Edwards, qtd. in Thorsson, "Foodways in Contemporary African American Poetry," 194.

21. Laretta Henderson, "'Ebony Jr!' And 'Soul Food': The Construction of Middle-Class African American Identity

through the Use of Traditional Southern Foodways," *MELUS* 32, no. 4 (2007), 81–97. Henderson's reading of collards, richly informed by scholars and poets including Amiri Baraka, is particularly illuminating as we can apply it to Mullen's tanka: "A term coined in the North, 'soul food,' was part of a self-defining discourse of the 1960s and 1970s. Some commentators, such as Amiri Baraka (then known as LeRoi Jones) 'began valorizing it as an expression of pride in the cultural forms created from and articulated through a history of black oppression.' Scholars define soul food in terms of three attributes: a connection to Africa and the diet of enslaved blacks, something inherent in the black body, and a tool to define a black identity (Baraka, Van Deburg, Witt). Van Deburg states that soul food originated in Western Africa and was transported to the American South with the slave trade. Baraka also used soul food to show connections within the African diaspora, whether it was ingredients such as black-eyed peas, collard greens, and okra, or cooking methods such as deep-fat frying. In *Black Hunger*, Doris Witt states that 'the emergence of soul food should be construed not just synchronically but also diachronically, as a part of an ongoing debate among African Americans over the appropriate food "practices" of blackness.' Soul food was encoded with blackness." (82)

22. Mullen, *Urban Tumbleweed*, 61.
23. Thorsson, "Foodways in Contemporary African American Poetry," 188.
24. Harryette Mullen, *Recyclopedia: Trimmings, S*PeRM**K*T, and Muse & Drudge* (Graywolf Press, 2006), 176.
25. Jennifer Reimer, "Disordering the Border: Harryette Mullen's Transaborder Poetics in *Muse & Drudge*," *ariel: A Review of International English Literature* 45, 172.
26. Thorsson, "Foodways in Contemporary African American Poetry," 189.
27. "Tanka Society of America – What Is Tanka?," accessed February 7, 2022: https://www.tankasocietyofamerica.org /essays/what-is-tanka
28. Mullen, *Urban Tumbleweed*, 17.
29. Bruce Ross, *Venturing Upon Dizzy Heights: Lectures and Essays on Philosophy, Literature, and the Arts* (Peter Lang, 2008), 106.
30. Mullen, *Urban Tumbleweed*, 21.

31. Ibid., 23.
32. Ibid., 27.
33. Ibid., 54.
34. Ibid., 73.
35. Hamilton, 132.
36. Mullen, *Urban Tumbleweed*, 7.
37. Ibid., 18.
38. Ibid., 20.
39. Ibid., 120.
40. Deborah Brown, Annie Finch, and Maxine Kumin, *Lofty Dogmas: Poets on Poetics* (University of Arkansas Press, 2005), 283.
41. Ibid., 21.

Notes on the Poems

Collected Poems 1981–1982

Blues Baby: Early Poems (1981–1982)

Five poems from *Blues Baby* (Bucknell University Press, 2002)
These poems were written in 1981–1982
'Of Two Minds'
'A Woman is Dreaming'
'Cartoon Men'
'You Who Walked Through the Fire'
'She Landed on the Moon'

Poetry Collections

Recyclopedia (2006)
   Trimmings (1991)
   S*PeRM**K*T (1992)
   Muse & Drudge (1995)
Recyclopedia (Graywolf Press 2006) collects three texts originally published by Tender Buttons Books and Singing Horse Press.

Sleeping with the Dictionary was first published by the University of California Press. The editor thanks the University of California Press for permission to reproduce the selection of poems republished in this volume.

Urban Tumbleweed: Notes From a Tanka Diary was first published by Graywolf Press in 2013. The editor thanks Graywolf for permissions to reproduce this volume.

Uncollected Poems 2001–2021

'Liberation of Ms. Liberty' (*WomEnhouse*, 1996)
   Harryette Mullen, from 'Porch', collaboration with visual artist
   Yong Soon Min, included in *WomEnhouse*, 1996; interactive
   feminist art project on website sponsored by Contemporary
   Museum of Photography at University of California, Riverside
   and UCLA Hammer Museum, 1996; documented in 'A Visit
   to WomEnhouse', Pat Morton, *Architecture of the Everyday*
   (Princeton Architectural Press, 2012), edited by Deborah
   Berkes and Steven Harris.
'The Fire This Time' (*Cave Canem Anthology*, Black Classics Press,
   2001)
'Poetry for Dummies' (*Callaloo*, 2001)
'Summer Salt' (*Callaloo*, 2001)
'Unacknowledged Legislator' (*Volt*, 2003; *Rainbow Darkness*,
   2005)
'Waving the Flag' (NewTown Arts, collaboration with Shelia M.
   Sofian and Will Darity, 2006)
   Waving the Flag (video animation by Sheila M. Sofian with
   words by Harryette Mullen), Waving the Flag: http://beta
   .newtownarts.org/shows/06_speaksee/index.php; https://vimeo
   .com/101966199

   Comment on 'Waving the Flag'
   'Following initial discussions with animation artist Sheila
   Sofian, I wrote "Waving the Flag," a twelve-stanza poem com-
   posed of a dozen variations on "The Pledge of Allegiance."
   As a U.S. citizen whose ancestors, all the way back to the
   American Revolution, have defended our country in war, I feel
   that what is most important to me is not the sign or emblem of
   patriotism, such as a banner or anthem, but the rights and free
   doms that these symbols represent. My allegiance is to demo-
   cratic values rather than to a flag. When it comes to defending
   American ideals, I am instructed by critical distinctions that
   Adrienne Rich articulated in her poem "The Burning of Paper
   Instead of Children," inspired by young men who burned their
   draft cards to protest the U.S. war in Vietnam. 'Waving the
   Flag' also is informed by a US Supreme Court decision over-
   turning laws that criminalised flag desecration, particularly in
   a case involving the artist Scott Tyler, known professionally as

Dread Scott, famous for his interactive art installation, 'What Is the Proper Way to Display a U.S. Flag'.

Sheila Sofian directed my performance in the animated video "Waving the Flag," and she created strong images that make the ideas more concrete and vivid. Accompanying the opening and closing credits of the video is a bluesy version of the national anthem performed on electric guitar by my nephew, Will Darity. My verses in "Waving the Flag" are indebted to Lee Ann Brown's "Pledge" from her poetry collection *Polyverse* (Sun & Moon Press, 1999). "Waving the Flag" also comments on the quintessentially American conflation of patriotism and consumerism that I explored previously in another poem, "Land of the Discount Price, Home of the Brand Name" published in the anthology *Is This Forever, or What?* edited by Naomi Shihab Nye (Greenwillow Books, 2004) (https://vimeo.com/101966199).'

'Sugar Land' (*Texas Observer*, 2007)

'Curious Strangers' (*Texas Observer*)

'Remove Offensive Language' (Fact-Smile Editions, Poet Trading Card, 2010)

'Antarctica' (Center for Book Arts, 2013)

'Broken Glish' (Center for Book Arts, 2013)

'Devil's Ashtray' (Center for Book Arts, 2013)

'Immaterial' (Center for Book Arts, 2013)

'Not Dead Yet' (Center for Book Arts, 2013)

"Blue herons persist" (*Harvard Review*, 2017; *Renga for Obama*, 2018)

'Barbaracrostics' (*Interim*, 2021)

'Y the Or' (*Interim*, 2021)

Contributors

Lee Ann Brown is Professor of English at St John's University, New York City. Lee Ann is the author of *Other Archer* (2015), *In the Laurels, Caught* (2013), *Crowns of Charlotte* (2013), *The Sleep That Changed Everything* (2003), and *Polyverse* (1999). Collaborative books and projects include *Bagatelles for Cornell* with Karen Randall (2012), *Sop Doll! A Jack Tale Noh* with Tony Torn (2009), *Nascent Toolbox* with Laynie Browne (2004), *The Thirteenth Sunday in Ordinary Time* (a Song Cycle), *Dia/Gnostic*, an artists' book with Anne Slacik (2001) and *The 3:15 Experiment* with Bernadette Mayer, Danika Dinsmore and Jen Hofer (2001). Recognition for her work includes two Firecracker Awards and the Lord Nose Award as editor and publisher of Tender Buttons Press, as well as fellowships for her own poetry from the New York Foundation for the Arts, the Howard Foundation Award, the Fund for Poetry and a Judith E. Wilson Visiting Poetry Fellowship at the University of Cambridge.

Solveig Daugaard's research field is modernist and contemporary American poetry, contemporary Scandinavian art and literature informed by affect and media theory and infrastructural studies. Her research and literary criticism have appeared in journals and papers in Denmark, Sweden and abroad. She is currently an assistant professor at the Department of Arts and Cultural Studies, University of Copenhagen. She is also active as an editor and as part of a translator collective translating the work of Gertrude Stein into Danish. Her PhD in Literature, Media History and Information Cultures is from Linköping University.

Alan Gilbert is the author of three books of poetry, *The Everyday Life of Design* (2020), *The Treatment of Monuments* (2012) and

491

Late in the Antenna Fields (2011). He is also the author of a collection of essays, articles and reviews entitled *Another Future: Poetry and Art in a Postmodern Twilight* (2006). He is the recipient of a 2019 Creative Capital | Andy Warhol Foundation Arts Writers Grant, a 2009 New York Foundation for the Arts Fellowship in Poetry and a 2006 Creative Capital Foundation Award for Innovative Literature. He is Adjunct Associate Professor in the Columbia University MFA writing programme and is the website editor for BOMB Magazine.

Emily Greenwood is James M. Rothenberg Professor of Classics and Comparative Literature at Harvard University. Her books include *Thucydides and the Shaping of History* (2006) and *Afro-Greeks: Dialogues Between Anglophone Caribbean Literature and Classics in the Twentieth Century* (2010). Recently she guest-edited a two-volume special issue of the *American Journal of Philology* entitled 'Diversifying Classical Philology' (issues 143.2 and 143.4). She is currently at work on two book projects: *Conjugating Black Classicisms* and *The Recovery of Loss: Classics and the Erasure of American Experiences*.

Daniel Kane is Professor of American literature at Uppsala University, Sweden. His publications include *All Poets Welcome: The Lower East Side Poetry Scene in the 1960s* (2003), *We Saw the Light: Conversations between the New American Cinema and Poetry* (2009) and *Do You Have a Band? Poetry and Punk Rock in New York City* (2017).

Ayesha Ramachandran is a literary critic and cultural historian of the early modern world. She is the author of *The Worldmakers* (2015) and has published essays on Renaissance literature, maps, cosmopolitanism, humanism, and global early modernity in various journals and collections. Currently she is Associate Professor of Comparative Literature at Yale University and is working on a book entitled, *Lyric Thinking: Towards a Global Poetics*.

Bibliography

Ahmed, Sara. *What's the Use? On the Uses of Use*. Durham, NC: Duke University Press, 2019.

Armand, Louis, ed. *Contemporary Poetics*. Evanston, IL: Northwestern University Press, 2007.

Bennett, Joshua. *Being Property Once Myself: Blackness and the End of Man*. Cambridge, MA: Belknap Press, 2020.

Brooks, Maegan Parker and Davis W. Houck, eds. *Speeches of Fannie Lou Hamer: To Tell It Like It Is*. Jackson: University Press of Mississippi, 2010.

Collins, Patricia Hill. *Black Feminist Thought: Knowledge, Consciousness, and the Poetics of Empowerment*, 2nd edition. New York: Routledge, 2000.

Cooper, Anna Julia. *A Voice from the South*. With an Introduction by Mary Helen Washington. New York: Oxford University Press, 1988.

Davis, Angela Yvonne. *Blues Legacies and Black Feminism: Gertrude "Ma" Rainey, Bessie Smith, and Billie Holliday*. New York: Pantheon Books, 1998.

Ellison, Ralph. 'The Little Man at Chehaw Station: The American Artist and his Audience'. *American Scholar* 47, no. 1 (Winter 1977–1978): 25–48.

Frost, Elisabeth. '"Ruses of the Lunatic Muse": Harryette Mullen and Lyric Hybridity'. *Women's Studies* 27 (1998): 465–481.

Frost, Elisabeth. *The Feminist Avant-Garde in American Poetry*. Iowa City: Iowa University Press, 2003.

Fuss, Diana. *Essentially Speaking: Feminism, Nature, and Difference*. New York: Routledge, 1989.

Griffin, Farah Jasmine. 'When Malindy Sings: A Meditation on Black Women's Vocality'. In *Uptown Conversations: The New Jazz Studies*, edited by Robert G. O'Meally, Brent Hayes

Edwards and Farah Jasmine Griffin, 102–125. New York: Columbia University Press, 2004.

Gubar, Susan. 'Sapphistries'. In *Reading Sappho: Reception and Transmission*, edited by Ellen Greene, 199–217. Berkeley: University of California Press, 1996.

Hart, Matthew. *Nations of Nothing But Poetry: Modernism, Transnationalism, and Synthetic Vernacular Writing*. New York: Oxford University Press, 2010.

Hartman, Saidiya. *Wayward Lives, Beautiful Experiments: Intimate Histories of Riotous Black Girls, Troublesome women, and Queer Radicals*. New York: W.W. Norton & Company, 2019.

Henderson, Mae Gwendolyn. 'Speaking in Tongues: Dialogics, Dialectics, and the Black Women Writer's Literary Tradition'. In *Changing Our Own Words: Essays on Criticism, Theory and Writing by Black Women*, edited by Cheryl A. Wall, 16–37. New Brunswick, NJ: Rutgers University Press, 1989.

Henning, Barbara. *Looking up Harryette Mullen: Interviews on Sleeping with the Dictionary and Other Works*. Introduction by Juliana Spahr. Brooklyn, NY: Belladonna Press, 2011.

Hopkins, Pauline. *Contending Forces: A Romance Illustrative of Negro Life North and South*. With an Introduction by Richard Yarborough. New York: Oxford University Press, 1988.

Hurston, Zora Neale. *Their Eyes Were Watching God: A Novel*. Philadelphia, PA: J. B. Lippincott, 1937.

Kennerly, Michele, ed. *A New Handbook of Rhetoric: Inverting the Classical Vocabulary*. University Park: Pennsylvania State University Press, 2021.

Lorde, Audre. *The Selected Works of Audre Lorde, Edited and With an Introduction by Roxane Gay*. New York: Norton, 2020.

Mackey, Nathaniel. 'Other: From Noun to Verb'. *Representations* 39 (Summer 1992): 51–70.

Mansell, Lisa. 'Hearing a New Musical Instrument: Harryette Mullen's Critical Lyricism'. In *Black Music, Black Poetry: Blues and Jazz's Impact on African American Versification*, edited by Gordon E. Thompson, 127–145. London and New York: Routledge, 2016.

Mix, Deborah M. 'Inspiration, Perspiration, and Impudence in Harryette Mullen's *Muse & Drudge*'. *Contemporary Women's Writing* 8, no. 1 (March 2014): 53–70.

Morton, Pat. 'A Visit to WomEnhouse'. In *Architecture of the*

Everyday, edited by Deborah Burke and Steven Harris. Princeton, NJ: Princeton Architectural Press/Yale Publications, 1997.

Moten, Fred and Stefano Harney. *The Undercommons. Fugitive Planning and Black Study*. Wivenhoe: Minor Compositions, 2013.

Mullen, Harryette. 'Imagining the Unimagined Reader: Writing to the Unborn and Including the Excluded'. *Boundary 2* 26, no. 1 (Spring 1999): 198–203.

Mullen, Haryette. *Sleeping with the Dictionary*. Berkeley: University of California Press, 2002.

Mullen, Haryette. *Recyclopedia: Trimmings, S*PeRM**K*T, and Muse & Drudge*. St. Paul, MN: Graywolf Press, 2006.

Mullen, Harryette. *The Cracks Between What We Are What We Are Supposed To Be: Essays and Interviews*. Introduction by Hank Lazer. Tuscaloosa: University of Alabama Press, 2012.

Perloff, Marjorie. 'After Language Poetry: Innovation and its Theoretical Discontents'. In *Contemporary Poetics*, edited by Louis Armand, 15–38. Evanston, IL: Northwestern University Press, 2007.

Philip, Marlene NourbeSe. *She Tries Her Tongue, Her Silence Softly Breaks*. 2nd edition. Middletown, CT: Wesleyan University Press, 2015.

Rayor, Diane J. *Sappho's Lyre. Archaic Lyric and Women Poets of Ancient Greece*. Translations, with Introductions and Notes, by Diane J. Rayor. Berkeley: University of California Press, 1991.

Rayor, Diane J. and William W. Batstone, eds. *Latin Lyric and Elegiac Poetry: An Anthology of New Translations*. New York: Garland, 1995.

Reed, Anthony. *Freedom Time: The Poetics and Politics of Black Experimental Writing*. Baltimore, MD: Johns Hopkins University Press, 2014.

Ross, Fran. *Oreo*. Reprint: With a New Introduction by Harryette Mullen. Boston, MA: Northeastern University Press, 2000.

Ryan, Jennifer D. *Post-Jazz Poetics: A Social History*. New York: Palgrave Macmillan, 2010.

Scroggins, Mark. *Intricate Thicket: Reading Late Modernist Poetries*. Tuscaloosa: University of Alabama Press, 2015.

Sharpe, Christina. *In the Wake: On Blackness and Being*. Durham, NC: Duke University Press, 2016.

Shockley, Evie. *Renegade Poetics: Black Aesthetics and Formal*

Innovation in African American Poetry. Iowa City: University of Iowa Press, 2011.

Smith, Barbara, ed. *Home Girls: A Black Feminist Anthology*. New York: Kitchen Table–Women of Color Press, 1983.

Spahr, Juliana. *Everybody's Autonomy: Connective Reading and Collective Identity*. Tuscaloosa: University of Alabama Press, 2001.

Taylor, Keeanga-Yamahtta, ed. *How we Get Free: Black Feminism and the Combahee River Collective*. Edited and introduced by Keeanga-Yamahtta Taylor. Chicago, IL: Haymarket Books, 2017.

Wall, Cheryl A., ed. *Changing Our Own Words: Essays on Criticism, Theory and Writing by Black Women*. New Brunswick, NJ: Rutgers University Press, 1989.

Winkler, John Jack. 'Gardens of Nymphs: Public and Private in Sappho's Lyrics'. In *Reading Sappho: Contemporary Approaches*, edited by Ellen Greene, 89–109. Berkeley: University of California Press, 1996.

EU representative:
Easy Access System Europe
Mustamäe tee 50, 10621 Tallinn, Estonia
Gpsr.requests@easproject.com

www.ingramcontent.com/pod-product-compliance
Lightning Source LLC
Chambersburg PA
CBHW051055030726
47504CB00006B/1643